After Hours

After Hours

Scorsese, Grief and the Grammar of
Cinema

(Auteur)

Ben Tanzer

PUBLISHING
New York, NY

Ig Publishing
Box 2547
New York, NY 10163
www.igpub.com

ISBN: 978-1-63246-17-11

PRINTED IN THE UNITED STATES OF AMERICA

For the artists who made me—past, present, and future.

"Oh my God, you're alive!"

This quote closes a 2021 interview with the actor Griffin Dunne. Titled "Griffin Dunne Answers Every Question We Have About *After Hours*," the interview ran as part of a series called "Reasons to Love New York—New York celebrates the city's timeless, peerless connection to movies."[1]

After Hours speaks to the sense of adventure and possibility that the city endlessly exudes. How New York is a character all its own. A place where people go to escape and pursue artistic dreams. To many, merely living in New York City is akin to the act of creation.

After Hours is also the movie that brought director Martin Scorsese's career back to life—and helped usher in my own. Well, *After Hours*, and *Naked Lunch* (the movie), the film *Short Cuts*, and *The Basketball Diaries*, (the book, not the movie.)

It's not just those cultural touchstones—which so many of us have some thoughts about—but also books by fellow authors and contemporaries such as *Excavation* by Wendy C. Ortiz and *Jacket Weather* by Mike DeCapite, works fractured and fragmented and drawing on memory, associations, journals, diaries. Tools I utilized when I moved to New York City in the early 1990s, hoping to build a life focused on creation. Tools I returned to thirty years later during the pandemic as I tried to figure out how one finds balance in a life now creative.

~

I grew up in a family where movies provided the lens into the where's and when's of who we were and what we were doing, as well as allowing us to make sense of those where's and when's.

My first movie? François Truffaut's *The Wild Child*—age two. After seeing the film, my therapist mother asked me what I thought it was about, and I replied, "the boy wanted to go home."

Isn't that the way it is with movies though? We want to escape something—drudgery, feeling trapped—and we want to return to something as well—calm, pleasure, a place that makes sense.

Which is what *After Hours* is about. An office drone named Paul Hackett, portrayed by Griffin Dunne, heads down to SoHo in New York City to briefly escape his redundant, insular, and boring life, and when he wants to go home, he can't find his way there, despite how hard he tries.

Is that description of the movie too simple or reductionist?

Of course.

Is it accurate?

Totally.

Why does it mean something to me?

You'll see.

One thing I know is that *After Hours*—and Martin Scorsese—meant something to my mother and my father, both New Yorkers and Jews, both cineastes.

My father is long dead now, which I share because this book is about a lot of things he cared about—*After Hours*, Scorsese, cinema's importance to our lives, creativity, genius, New York City, chaos, balance, memory, living an artistic life where one feels some kind of control over their destiny—none of which Paul Hackett feels, nor what Scorsese felt when he decided to make the film.

This work is also about grief—how it never goes away, and how we adapt to loss by simultaneously embracing it and pushing through it—something I want to believe can be as organic as anything I'm attempting here.

~

From the beginning of my literary life I've had a blog called "This Blog Will Change Your Life." It was something I embarked on as part of a larger and then nascent literary movement to utilize social media to accomplish...what exactly? For me, it was an effort to draw attention to my work and the work of other authors I admired. I was self-conscious about being quite so public with my musings, yearnings, and desperation, yet not so self-conscious that I was willing to risk missing whatever might happen, or any potential opportunities for promotion.

My strategy for embracing these possibilities was to write a faux corporate blog where my work would be presented and marketed by a much larger creative enterprise known as TBWCYL, Inc. It was successful and slowly found an audience over time.

In November 2007 I read that the author Jonathan Lethem had been invited to curate a film festival, and I wondered which movies I might choose if given the same opportunity. I posted the following line-up to my blog:

1. *After Hours*
2. *Hoop Dreams*
3. *Apocalypse Now*

4. *Punch Drunk Love*

5. *Niagara, Niagara*

6. *Once Were Warriors*

7. *Barfly*

8. *American History X*

9. *Caddyshack*

10. *Short Cuts*

11. *The Squid and the Whale*

12. *Alien*

13. *Swingers*

14. *One False Move*

15. *Reservoir Dogs*

16. *Dead Man*

17. *In the Company of Men*

18. *Escape from New York*

19. *Do The Right Thing*

20. *In the Bedroom*

21. *Barton Fink*

22. *Kids*

23. *The Breakfast Club*

24. *Requiem for a Dream*

25. *The Warriors*

26. *Boys Don't Cry*

27.   *Drugstore Cowboy*
28.   *Die Hard* *

These movies complemented the themes I explored
and still explore in my work—damaged people, fractured
families, the threat of violence, oppression, adultery, sexuality,
substance abuse, etc. Many of my characters don't have the

---

* I'm not sure how I allowed myself to leave *Blade Runner* off
this list, except that I felt no director ought to be included
more than once (how else would *The Godfather* be absent) and
Ridley Scott also directed *Alien*—a movie as formative to my
childhood as any. Still, it's *Blade Runner* and it would replace
Alien on the list today—and *Ghost Dog: Way of the Samurai*
would take *Dead Man's* place. Where *Brazil* is, as well as *Naked
Lunch* and *Mysterious Skin*, escapes and infuriates me—chalk
those up to massive oversights.

There are also movies which came later that cannot be
ignored now: *Boyhood* certainly, though it would be hard to leave
Before Midnight off the list, and like *Brazil*, I have no idea how
it wasn't on the original list regardless. There are also *The Florida
Project. Fruitvale Station. Logan. Uncut Gems, The 40-year-Old
Virgin. Mad Max: Fury Road. Minding the Gap. Moonlight. OJ:
Made in America. Shoplifters. Winter's Bone.* Maybe *Scott Pilgrim
vs. The World*, which my younger son Noah loves.

It all starts with *After Hours*, however, and always has.

self-awareness, support, coping skills or decision-making abilities to communicate about, much less fully grasp, how to handle or make sense of the situations and relationships they find themselves in. Sometimes these characters persevere; sometimes they don't. They're also predominantly male and share a lot of traits with Paul Hackett—they want to feel alive and yet so many things, such as their own limitations and fears especially, conspire against their desire to do so with equanimity or calm.

~

At some point in the 1990s—well after *After Hours* was released in 1985 and somewhat after *Goodfellas* in 1990, though well before *The Departed* in 2006, which is not bad, *The Wolf of Wall Street* in 2013, which is quite fun, and *The Irishman* in 2019, which I enjoyed—I asked my father what we should make of Scorsese. Which is to say whether he thought he was done creating the kind of transcendent work we loved. My father responded, "how many masterpieces does someone need to make?" We didn't discuss what my father considered Scorsese's masterpieces, though I knew for both him and my mother it was *Mean Streets* (1973), *Taxi Driver* (1976), and *Raging Bull* (1980). *Goodfellas* and *The King of Comedy* (1982) were also part of the conversation. *The Last Temptation of Christ* (1988) didn't quite fall into this debate, though my parents both found it powerful and important—even if my father couldn't quite get past Harvey Keitel playing Judas with a Brooklyn accent.

Still, *The Last Temptation of Christ* is crucial to any discussion of *After Hours*. As described in *Esquire* upon the thirty-fifth anniversary of *After Hours*, "there was a time back in the early 1980's when Scorsese was written off as box-office poison." As Scorsese himself says in the article, "I had the TV on in the background and for some reason it was tuned to *Entertainment Tonight*. And I heard them say as sort of a tease before they went to commercial, 'Coming up: The Movie Flop of the Year!' So I sort of stuck around to see what it was. What was the Movie Flop of the Year? And when they came back, they said it was *The King of Comedy*! I was the flop of the year! And on top of that, I had been planning to make *The Last Temptation of Christ*, which had just been canceled on me. So it was a double whammy. I had nothing lined up next. And I knew I was going to have to start all over." [2]

Scorsese's next movie after the "flop of the year" would be *After Hours*.

~

After Hours is about the desire to escape the cubicle life: meaning structure, stability, predictability. I didn't grow up like that. In my house, there were no rules—or not many— or expectations, beyond being a decent person, becoming an activist, and seeking out work—always work. My parents were people engaged with the world and focused on their relationship, art, and travel. They weren't always present, but there wasn't much for me to escape from.

On Friday nights, we would eat dinner at Little Venice Restaurant in downtown Binghamton, New York, where I grew up. Those dinners were often followed by us going to the movies. As I got older, we watched movies together less often, though I was still likely to see films my parents recommended. These included:

The King of Comedy.

Little Odessa. My father recommended it, though my mother believes she did as well. Anyway, it was New York City and Russian Jewish mobsters, and my dad loved New York City and mobsters. Years later I met James Gray, the writer/ director of the movie, and when I told him how much my father and I had enjoyed it, he replied, "and you're the only two people who've ever seen it."

She's Gotta Have It. My father had a habit of seeing movies before I did and then telling me to see them. He liked this one and made sure I knew it.

The Shining. I loved Stephen King's books then and loved this movie—not that Stephen King did. It doesn't speak to my experience as a writer, though it didn't scare me off either. I consider that a win.

Body Double and *Body Heat.* The latter starred the still young William Hurt and Kathleen Turner, as well as Mickey Rourke and Ted Danson. *Body Double* stars Melanie Griffith and Craig Wasson. Both are about obsession and anything about obsession is good with me.

One False Move. So much violence and dread, plus Billy Bob Thorton and Bill Paxton.

Something Wild. More Melanie Griffith and more violence. It also co-stars Ray Liotta in a truly incendiary breakout performance.

And of course, *After Hours*.

~

A key conceit to *After Hours* is the sense that it could only happen in New York City. Especially during the 1980s, the city was the perfect mélange of weirdness, dislocation, art, and potential violence. However, I was never scared of New York—in part because I wasn't raised to fear the city. In the 1970s and 1980s, my parents and I would visit my grandmother in Queens. We would all eat chopped liver on Ritz crackers and see Broadway shows—including the original runs of *Grease* and *Sweeney Todd*. I attended my first professional baseball game at the original Yankee Stadium, mere blocks from the neighborhood where my father grew up.

These are childhood memories, though. I also lived in the city as an adult from 1992 to 1994. I have numerous reminiscences from those years too, including:

- Tripping on mushrooms at Webster Hall on East 11th, then walking the empty streets and being passed by a pack of rats—who then beelined down a deserted alley.

- Having drinks at the original Max Fish on Ludlow Street after being informed beforehand that if we took the correct turn off the train, we'd easily find it and if we took the wrong turn we'd walk into a drug deal. We took a wrong turn, and yes, walked into a drug deal.

- Eating pâté in the early morning with the queens and club kids at Florent in the Meatpacking District on the way home from wherever we were and not yet ready for bed.

- Getting home late one New Year's Eve to an answering machine message that we were invited to a party at Parker Posey's. The message was from Adam Lawrence, another childhood friend of mine, who knew her from college.

- Hitting CBGB to watch Monkey Wrench fronted by Tim Walikas, a friend of mine since middle school.

- Volunteering at Gay Men's Health Crisis to raise money and support for the AIDS Walk and HIV/AIDS research and programming.

- Discovering the work of Jean-Michel Basquiat at his first post-death retrospective at the Whitney Museum of American Art.

- Feeling terrorized by a neighbor on West 96th Street who wandered the building and our neighborhood with a hunting knife and pit bull whose mouth was sealed with duct tape. He would eventually blow-up his apartment, which he told the police I was responsible for, and set our building's elevator on fire.

- Working in Long Island City during the first World Trade Center bombing and watching the smoke ascend into the sky from my office window.

- Getting assaulted on a sunny Friday afternoon on West 125th Street in Harlem—the entire incident lasting two minutes, the scar bisecting my eyebrow permanent.

~

What wasn't happening when I moved to New York City was writing. While living in San Francisco from 1990 to 1992, I'd decided I had no choice but to somehow become a writer. I had not. Instead, I watched a lot of movies:

Paris is Burning. A documentary about a New York City I never knew existed.

Silence of the Lambs. I watched this on a random Saturday afternoon, alone and spellbound.

Faces. Another Saturday and a movie and director—John Cassavetes—that my parents—and Scorsese—loved.

Goodfellas. With friends on a Friday night, Scorsese's career resurgence firmly afoot.

The Doors and *JFK.* These both follow the wholly engrossing *Born on the Fourth of July*, and while entertaining, are not quite great, and represent a sort of endpoint to Oliver Stone's terrific run of moviemaking. Of course, how many masterpieces does one need to create?

Edward Scissorhands. I watched this on Christmas Eve with my father, while my mother and uncle watched Havana. We won the movies that night!

Thelma & Louise. I saw this with a former friend, and it was like nothing we'd ever seen before.

L.A. Story. I saw this quite high in Oakland, the pleasures bountiful.

Barfly. A late-night rental with a different former friend who insisted we had to watch it as we quaffed Jack & Gingers into the early morning. My first exposure to anything Bukowski.

Naked Lunch. Very late at night, lots of friends. I was mesmerized, inspired, filled with nervous energy and glee, and wondering when I would start writing.

~

From 1990—when I graduated from college—through 2016, I worked nine to five. While I was never quite an office drone, I did work in offices, with bosses, trainings, human resources, supervision, repetition, interviews, salary negotiations, cubicles, countless co-workers—some good, some bad, most indifferent—endless meetings, retreats, conferences, planning sessions, expense reports, invoices, flights, hotel rooms, per diems, and on and on. I craved structure, stability, regular paychecks, health insurance, and retirement plans. I was never quite Paul Hackett, yet my life was much closer to his than that of my parents. My father worked at IBM for one day in his early twenties and never entered an office again. My mother worked in a mental health clinic when we first moved to Binghamton, but it didn't stick, and she went into private practice. She ascribed this decision to poor management at the clinic, though this doesn't change who she is, or my father was—people who followed rules yet needed to make their own, and who sought comfort, but not at the expense of forging their own paths, which were unrestricted and well outside the confines of institutions.

I wasn't that guy.

~

As we have established, the creation of *After Hours* emerged from Scorsese's initial inability to get *The Last Temptation of Christ* made. As the director says in the commentary for the *After Hours* DVD: "And so this film (…) comes out of a feeling of being stuck in the underworld and never being able to get out, maybe never being able to get to make another big film in a sense or does one just continue. There's no such thing as a big film, it's just a film, whether it's 20 million, 100 million, 5 million, 100 thousand. It's still gotta sell emotions, gotta sell ideas. So, think about how you could sustain yourself creatively…"

Film critic Koraljka Suton adds to this relationship between the two films—and Franz Kafka—writing that:

> This Kafkaesque notion of being stuck inside an absurd system without any means of getting out is indeed one that permeates the entirety of Scorsese's wonderfully crafted movie, for Paul cannot escape SoHo no matter how hard he tries and the circumstances of his "captivity" keep getting more absurd by the minute. A dialogue between Paul and a doorman at a club he wants to enter, as well as a scene between the protagonist and a tollbooth operator in a subway, are directly inspired by Kafka's work, reflecting Scorsese's own process of waiting for the production of *The Last Temptation of Christ* and his frustration due to the ultimate futility of it all.[3]

What is Kafka's work, *After Hours*, and Scorsese's career if not an exploration of the act of creation. Also, what does it mean that my father became focused on Kafka—his Jewishness and outsiderness—after I asked him to illustrate the college honors thesis I wrote on Kafka and the psychoanalytic underpinnings of his major works?

~

Does it mean something that Scorsese was interviewed in Deadline in 2023 in relation to the release of *Killers of the Flower Moon* and had the following exchange:[4]

> DEADLINE: You're 80. Do you still have that fire to get right back behind the camera and get the next one going?
>
> SCORSESE: Got to. Got to. Yeah. I wish I could take a break for eight weeks and make a film at the same time [laughs]. The whole world has opened up to me, but it's too late. It's too late.
>
> DEADLINE: What do you mean by that?
>
> SCORSESE: I'm old. I read stuff. I see things. I want to tell stories, and there's no more time. Kurosawa, when he got his Oscar, when George [Lucas] and Steven [Spielberg] gave it to him, he said, "I'm only now beginning to see the possibility of what cinema

could be, and it's too late." He was 83. At the time, I said, "What does he mean?" Now I know what he means.

To create.

To escape.

To live a creative life, we must live long enough to accomplish these things.

Scorsese is eighty.

Kafka was forty-one when he died.

My father was fifty-nine.

I'm fifty-four at the time of this writing.

How many masterpieces does one have to create?

The answer is there's never enough time.

One day near the end of my father's life, a young rebbe, his daughters and one of his followers came to the hospital to perform a Rosh Hashanah service. As the girls sang and the follower blew the shofar, my father silently cried. He hardly ever cried during his lifetime—too proud, too tightly wrapped in emotions, fears, and limitations. After the service my mother asked me if I thought my father might've been better able to stretch himself as an artist if he hadn't been so trapped in his own head. We won't know the answer to this, just as we won't know what comes next for Paul Hackett at the end of *After Hours* as he goes back to work.

~

There are a group of movies I associate with my father's death (though writing this now, I realize that I need to also craft a list of movies I associate with his life):

The Sixth Sense. We went to see this movie the first time I visited my father following his diagnosis with myelodysplasia and being given eighteen months to live if they couldn't find a bone marrow donor match. During the first hour of the movie, I was as full of dread as I've ever been. So much death, so fraught—how could my father sit through this? Further, what sort of trauma had the protagonist experienced and how would it be exposed? My chest tightened; the back of my neck bunched up. I wasn't sure I could bear it. And then, spoiler alert: the protagonist was merely seeing dead people. Who cares?

Hurricane. My father, mother, my wife Debbie, and I saw this together and then returned to my parents' house where we listened to the Dylan song on the original vinyl record my parents had purchased back in the 1970s. The mood was languorous and relaxed.

Dancer in the Dark. I loathe to say that watching any movie is a mistake, though if *The Sixth Sense* flinched when it could have destroyed, *Dancer in the Dark* refused to flinch or turn away from the encroaching horror on the screen, inching along in a slow, brutal march towards certain death.

The Original Kings of Comedy. My father was in the hospital when this came out and did not leave again. My mother had barely left the hospital herself, so I took her out to the movies one day. If Scorsese is the throughline in the arc of our familial cinematic experiences, Spike Lee runs adjacent, and in this case my mother and I enjoyed the stand-up stylings of Cedric the Entertainer, Bernie Mac, Steve Harvey, and D.L. Hughley. After the movie I went to the hospital. My father's temperature had spiked so high he'd been placed on an ice-cold mat to cool him down—he was so chilled the bones shook under his emaciated frame.

Dr. T & The Women. Is there such a thing as a not great Robert

Altman movie? The answer is yes. Debbie and I went to see this after we returned to Chicago following my father's funeral. It was a particularly unfortunate and boring choice and watching it felt like blasphemy in the wake of my father's loss.

Frequency. I don't know if *Frequency is better* than *Dr. T & The Women*, but what I do know is that Jim Caviezel plays a drunken cop who connects across time with his long dead fireman father played by Dennis Quaid on their old ham radio and is able to first converse with him, before trying to save his life—in the past—which he does! I cry bullshit on that. Even though my father felt strongly that moviegoers must be willing to suspend belief, we don't get our dead fathers back. I can write this today, clear-eyed and cogently—when I saw the movie just weeks after my father's death, I sobbed with such intensity Debbie was concerned for my mental health.

Ghost Dog: The Way of the Samurai. My father loved Jim Jarmusch, as well as all things crime, indie, and/or Japanese, and Forest Whitaker—my father once told me Whitaker had sad eyes. He would have loved this movie, but didn't live long enough to see it, so I watched it without him—the first of many.

Pollock. Should I have seen this movie with my mother just months after my father died? Doubtful.

Magnolia. My father loved Paul Thomas Anderson's first film, *Hard Eight*, but didn't make it to the release of *Magnolia*, with its heavy father shit. I saw it with Debbie and my co-workers one night when it was raining frogs on the streets of LA. Philip Seymour Hoffman was in it, as was Jason Robards and Philip Baker Hall, all dead now—and Tom Cruise's character at his long-estranged father's deathbed, hoping for some kind of moment, reconciliation, etc. As I sat there, I thought, how many of us find any resolution at our parent's deathbed? Still, while it may just be a movie thing, damn eit if it doesn't work every time.

Castaway. Debbie and I were talking about having a baby, something we deferred while my father was sick. I had suggested we take a trip together first, a moment to escape, one last adventure. "You go," she replied, "I'm good." I went to Italy. Just before that we'd gone to Joshua Tree with my mother, where we saw *Castaway* in an empty movie theater off a nearly deserted desert highway. Why do I share this? Because when I was in Florence months later eating dinner by myself, a man who looked much too much like my father—something about his clothes and unkempt hair, and something that happens when you lose someone—said, "Excuse me, you're American, no?" (My father always ended sentences with "no?") "Yes," I replied. "Did you see this *Castaway*?" "I did." "It's a good film, but it's not cinema, no?" "No." It isn't. Something I know my father would agree with.

~

Paul Hackett doesn't lead an artistic life. My father did and was able to do so in part because my mother worked and supported him. Did Kafka lead an artistic life? He obtained a Doctor of Law degree in 1906 and then spent a year where he was obligated to work as an unpaid law clerk in criminal and civil courts. In 1907 he began working in an Italian insurance company. He was unhappy with his work hours—8pm to 6am—as they interfered with his writing. In 1908 he found a job at the Worker's Accident Insurance Institute for the Kingdom of Bohemia, where he was employed until 1922, when he retired for health reasons. He referred to this work as a "bread job," which allowed him to pay the bills. Kafka died in 1924.

Kafka's story "A Hunger Artist"—a favorite of my father's—is the tale of a circus performer whose art is fasting—sitting in rags for forty days, observed by crowds, and engaged in the act of being, isolation, and asceticism. The hunger artist has fame yet feels misunderstood. When his public adulation begins to fade, he is placed in a cage and moved to the outskirts of the circus, where he's forgotten. Later, what seems to be a perfectly good cage is discovered to be going unused, until someone realizes the hunger artist is inside. They find him near death. The hunger artist asks that he not be admired for his art—he had to fast because he could never find any food he enjoyed. He soon dies, and is replaced by a young panther who's beloved by the crowds.

What Kafka was attempting to capture with "A Hunger Artist" was his belief that "[w]hat we need are books that affect us like some really grievous misfortune, like the death of one whom we loved more than ourselves, as if we were banished to distant forests, away from everybody, like a suicide; a book must be the ax for the frozen sea within us."[5] In other words, literature must make us feel.

This was also Scorsese's concern with the Marvel cinematic

universe:

> The only time his ardour dims is when the subject
> of Marvel comes up. "I don't see them," he says of
> the MCU. "I tried, you know? But that's not cinema.
> Honestly, the closest I can think of them, as well-
> made as they are, with actors doing the best they can
> under the circumstances, is theme parks. It isn't the
> cinema of human beings trying to convey emotional,
> psychological experiences to another human being.[6]

Scorsese is questioning how one can feel anything when watching an MCU movie. He, however, seeks to make us feel things with his movies. He wants his work to be that ax. He's also fighting against being pushed to the outskirts of the circus. Before *After Hours* was released, it wasn't clear if Scorsese was going to continue being given this opportunity. But after the film came out—and we *felt* something—this was no longer a question for him.

Scorsese has swung his ax ever since.

~

Does it mean something that I went to see *Guardians of the Galaxy, Vol. 3* on the same day that Scorsese's film, *Killers of the*

Flower Moon, debuted at Cannes? Was doing so a repudiation of Scorsese's position on Marvel movies? Does it matter that the *Guardians* films are not concerned with normal Marvel fare but instead are more focused on humor and what makes us human. Though like all Marvel movies, they also feature misfits and outsiders forming new families, something Scorsese is familiar with, though his cinematic family members frequently turn on one another to protect the larger family. Look no further than *Goodfellas*—Joe Pesci's character, Tommy DeVito, who the family kills when he becomes a problem, or Ray Liotta's character, Henry Hill, who rats on the family to save his own ass. Neither of those things would happen in a *Guardians* movie. If anything, people will sacrifice themselves for their families, if need be.

Yet, despite his emphasis on family, from *Taxi Driver* to *The Aviator* to *The Wolf of Wall Street*, Scorsese has also focused on individuals who fight the system, themselves, and especially the absurdity of modern life, which in turn bastardizes and warps everything it touches. This is never more the case than in *After Hours*.

~

In 2015, "Taste of Cinema" posted a piece called "The 10 Best

Movies Influenced by Franz Kafka."[7] I'll touch on some of their choices:

- Number Nine is *Eyes Wide Shut* by Stanley Kubrick, which they call a "serious and distorted" version of *After Hours* with a similar instigating event: a man goes where he should not, meeting characters both disturbing and disturbed. Kafka's impact can be seen both in the screenplay and the book the movie was inspired by— *Traumnovelle* by Arthur Schnitzler. Debbie and I passionately awaited the release of *Eyes Wide Shut*. It was a hot mess. It was also delightful.

- Number Eight is *Shadows and Fog* by Woody Allen. Sigh. I'm happy to keep my comments on Woody Allen to a minimum, but I don't want to skip this description of the movie, an arguably meta discussion of how Allen has conducted his life, creative and otherwise: "The normal person that is reluctantly forced to run from everyone, involved in things that are too much for him, the strange situations...and an ambiguous ending, deliberately incomplete and surrealistic, contribute to a mocking, funny and tragic atmosphere." Enough said.

- Number Five is *Brazil* by Terry Gilliam, which features bureaucracy, systems run amuck and Robert De Niro. How this wasn't on my original film festival list remains a criminal oversight.

- Number Four is *The Tenant* by Roman Polanski. This is the most terrifying movie on the list. It combines private madness and a Kafka-like protagonist who is a victim of events happening around him. I don't want to comment on Polanski anymore than I want to comment on Allen, though I just finished *Monsters: A Fan's Dilemma* by Claire Dederer, and her thoughtful take on whether we need to separate the art from the artist—we respond to what we respond to—which is Allenesque in its reasoning, certainly complicates my complicated feelings about both directors.

- Number One is...*After Hours*. To quote the article: "Scorsese updates Kafka to our postmodern times, to neon lights, to modern life, without losing its spirit and rendering it funny. The only way to survive life is to smile at it, no matter what is happening to you. At the end, you are going to be on time at work, returned to the society. Happy ending?"

~

One element of *After Hours* I continually return to is how it shows that capitalism seems to require structure and entrapment, and what that means for living a creative life. Kafka had to go to work. My father didn't, even if he worked—running frame and tattoo shops and teaching.

For much of my adult life, I gladly pursued a stable, nine to five existence where I was certain to have a steady paycheck, structure, health insurance, and the opportunity to save money for retirement, things my father—and to some extent my mother—eschewed, a decision which somewhat rejected my father's life choices.

When I began to write at the age of thirty, my mother asked me why it took me so long to start. She said, "You lived with an artist. You had a model." I didn't think of my father as such when I was growing up. He was my father, not an artist. Yet, it's more than that, too. His relationship with art represented a suffering that didn't appeal to me. It was one filled with great heights, but also frustration, disappointment, and failure. Not a failure to create; he could always create.

It was the failure to have more people, important people—gallery owners and museum curators in particular—care about his work. The Paul Hackett life choice felt far more appealing to me back then.

In his essay, "Michael Tanzer: An Artist Searching for His Routes," Albert Boime—an acclaimed art historian, a friend of my father's, and father of my long-time friend Eric Boime—quotes an interview my wife Debbie and I conducted with my father when he was dying. In the interview, my father speaks about the immigrant experience, something he strongly identified with, which emerged as we discussed Kafka with him. Boime wrote that, "Kafka's personal sense of alienation and simultaneous conflict of suppression and expression of his Jewish identity was vividly inscribed in his narrative of social and political estrangement." He then quoted my father, who said his roots, "should be thought of more as 'trade routes' or 'travel routes'" if one were to capture the existential substance of Jewish exile. Boime follows this with, "Tanzer's ingenious play on words speaks profoundly to his own tenuous sense of place in the heart of his native land. His works are saturated with allusions of social alienation, marginalization, memories, travels, and dreamy gazing."[8] This description of my father's work not only speaks to Kafka, but also the very foundations of

After Hours—the tenuous sense of place, the social alienation, travel, and dreamy gazing.

~

My father stopped creating near the end of his life, though he did work on a cover for a children's book I had written. He initially said he couldn't paint the cover because he was stuck and couldn't produce anything. When I asked why, he replied that he couldn't bear to leave the family with any more work. We would've been happy to be left with more work.

Can art save lives? It didn't save my father's, or Kafka—both of whom died young. But it did save Scorsese's life. Prior to *After Hours*, *The King of Comedy* "had flopped"—Scorsese's words—and *The Last Temptation of Christ* had lost its financial support. As Scorsese said in *Esquire*: "I knew I was going to start all over."

When one is engaged in writing about grief, as I would suggest I'm doing here, are we not starting over in some sense? There is a death, and then there is seeking to discern some sort of insight we can't quite grasp. The person we love is gone. How do we find traction in the new and confusing world we live in afterwards? If one is creative, you create something. The question is what's the proper lens for processing and reflecting on what we're trying to understand?

For me it's a book about *After Hours*.

INTERVIEW with Adam Tanzer

Ben Tanzer: Would you mind introducing yourself?

Adam Tanzer: Adam Tanzer, brother of Ben Tanzer.

BT: I want to start by asking about your relationship with movies.

AT: Movies have a real effect on me, but in somewhat inarticulate ways. For instance, I remember when I was sixteen and saw *The Graduate*. It was the first movie that was so unusual and exciting to me that after my friends and I watched it, I took the VHS home and rewatched it a second time the same night. I had never done that before. It engaged me in a way that people normally talk about novels—they get lost in it, there's an escapist quality and kind of entering this whole other world.

BT: I think about our family's relationship with movies as guideposts for delineating our time together and how we remember things. I'm curious about your take on that, as well as how our family felt about Scorsese.

AT: I remember when *Raging Bull* came out in 1980 and Mom took us to see the film in New York City. At ten years old, there was a lot I didn't appreciate, and I don't even know if I necessarily enjoyed the movie, as it was in black and white and dealt with adult themes. But seeing that movie at such a young age certainly left the impression that Scorsese was a serious artist, and that this was the kind of movies Mom and Dad prioritized seeing in New York, where there were all these different options. I wanted to like Scorsese because Mom and Dad held him in such high esteem.

BT: I know you're familiar with *After Hours*. How does it make you feel, and what do you think Scorsese was trying to do?

AT: I had never heard of the movie before seeing it late one night on HBO or something. I didn't know it was Scorsese. It was so weird, almost kind of cartoonish, or at least there was an over-the-top surrealist quality that I thought, at first, well this is what you get on HBO at two o'clock in the morning. I didn't take it seriously at first. Then as the movie went on, I thought, this is great! When I found out it was Scorsese, I appreciated it so much more since I had gone into the film without knowing it was him. Then I thought, this isn't just me emulating Mom and Dad. It was a good feeling to be like, oh, I really love this movie, and I discovered it in what felt like a less kind of biased way.

Since then, I've seen it many times, and, as with any great piece of art, it is different each time you see it because you are not the same. I feel that a critical part of the movie is at the end when Paul Hackett dances with the woman [June] to the song, "Is That All There Is?" That scene really hits me hard because there was so much energy going on and now there's this song and it's slow. It was such a shift in mood. To me, the Rosetta Stone of the movie is the song. Because when the movie starts, Paul Hackett has this goal of being an adult, he's this professional working in Manhattan. He looks good, his job is respectable. He starts off in this very conventional way, but then the question becomes why does he go on with his adventure? Why does he feel that he needs to have a change or a break? Then of course the movie ends and he's back at his office. I think that at a young age, there may have been that sense of, alright, I'm working hard for a certain goal, which is to get into the best college so I can have the best career possible. And I was really focused on that, that I had to go to a great school, then I'm going to have a great career, then I'm going to be happy. And what threw me off track was that Paul Hackett is in a sense a guy who went to a very good school, had a very good career, and I think that the song is about the idea that in late-stage capitalism, we're all kind of fed this myth of what the good life looks like. And I bought into it 100 percent. What was exciting about the movie was that this guy was leaving that conventionality.

~

My mother once asked me why I always write about my father and not her. A valid question. My immediate response was, "because you're alive." She seemed to appreciate, if not understand, that. But did I understand it? Was it, "I don't have to work through things on the page because you're here to work through them in person?" Or was it that Dad was taken too soon, and I'm caught in a perpetual cycle of grief I can never quite make sense of? Or could it be, "how can I say or imply things about you as I do him when you're here to respond and react to them?"

So, my mother.

She too loves *After Hours* and movies—period. She too has thoughts on Scorsese. And she most certainly has insights on the psychological underpinnings of *After Hours*, Kafka's writing, and anything else one cares to reflect on. My father was an artist and she's a therapist. I'm a product of both. Yet, can I write about her? I recently listened to an interview with a writing coach who knows David Chase, and he was asked, how does a guy who wrote for *The Rockford Files* go on to create *The Sopranos*? The coach replied, how else—his mother died, and he was liberated. I read something similar pertaining to Steven Spielberg and *The Fabelmans*. Why was Spielberg finally ready to write such a personal movie? His mother had finally died at ninety-seven. After watching *The Fabelmans*, I wondered what book I might write if my mother died—not that there's any rush. I sketched out a whole novel that may never see the light of day. There remains the question, though, about the relationship between one's creative life and being liberated from their parent's grip, if not shadow—even if you love them and they love you, as has always been my situation.

Sometimes, however, we know we're trapped, and we allow ourselves to feel it. We then say *what the fuck* and seek to liberate ourselves. When we do, the experience can feel quite like that of Paul Hackett's. It's thrilling at first, then scary and slightly out of control, if not desperate—wondering if we can get through it, maybe questioning who we are, before the situation rights itself and we're forced to decide if we intend to return to our same, safer path—or not. These are questions any of us might find ourselves asking as we move through life, especially when trying to find our voice as artists—or rediscover it, as Scorsese had to do—or when we're grieving.

~

Right, so I'm holding onto grief, as if I'm able to make a different life choice. What would such a choice look like, anyway? Maybe trying to understand Scorsese through the lens of grief? Where does that take you? Would you be surprised if I said The Ringer? The Ringer is a sports and pop culture site, and pop culture tells us there are five stages of grief, according to the work of Swiss psychologist Elisabeth Kübler-Ross—Denial, Anger, Bargaining, Depression, and Acceptance. It may be worth stating that this model has been subject to debate and criticism over the years, due to the belief that people grieve in a linear order while going through the stages—Kübler-Ross later said the stages aren't linear and some people may not experience any of them.

This seems important, though maybe not to The Ringer, which in December 2016 took this trope as a leaping off point to explore "The Five Stages of Scorsese," subtitled, "A decade-by-decade walk through the films of Martin Scorsese, the best 50-year director ever."[9] Not the best director per se, but the best for that extended timeframe. The article, written by Sean Fennessey, is briefly prefaced with commentary on Scorsese's first film, 1967's *Who's That Knocking at My Door*, released when Scorsese was twenty-five and about which fellow twenty-five-year-old Roger Ebert wrote, "I have no reservations describing it as a great moment in American movies." Ebert went on to say that the movie could be described as French New Wave meets documentary-style technique kissed with "ingenious bursts of musical interpolation."[10]

And so what are the five phases of Scorsese?

- 1967 to 1975: **The Come-up, aka "It's All Bullshit Except the Pain,"** comprised of *Who's That Knocking at My Door* (1967); *Street Scenes* (1970); *Boxcar Bertha* (1972); *Mean Streets* (1973); *Alice Doesn't Live Here Anymore* (1974); and *Italianamerican* (1974). The inspiration to write *Mean Streets* is noted as the result of John Cassavetes telling Scorsese that *Boxcar Bertha* was "a piece of shit."

- 1976 to 1983: **The Fury, aka "Screwheads,"** comprised of *Taxi Driver* (1976); *New York, New York* (1977); *The Last Waltz* (1978); *American Boy: A Profile of Steven Prince* (1978); *Raging Bull* (1980); and *The King of Comedy* (1983). Fennessey calls this "[m]aybe the single greatest five-movie run in cinema history?" He also stresses the "pure kinetic energy" of the movies and compares them to a "cocaine binge."

- 1985 to 1989: **The Wilderness, aka "Money Won Is Twice As Sweet As Money Earned,"** comprised of *After Hours* (1985); *The Color of Money* (1986); *"Mirror, Mirror"* (from *Amazing Stories*) (1986); *"Bad"* (Michael Jackson video) (1987); *The Last Temptation of Christ* (1988); *"Life Lessons"* (from *New York Stories*) (1989). The question posed about this stage is whether it involves "cash-grabs" to build equity. Fennessey stresses that *After Hours* is a "dystopian comedy" set on Scorsese's old stomping grounds, the Lower East Side, and chooses to focus on "Life Lessons," a short work which stars Nick Nolte as a Jackson Pollock-esque painter.

  This period is the re-boot, re-invention, and re-birth

of Scorsese as auteur, which *After Hours* kicks off as a kind of bridge, a burst of displacement and confused energy, emerging during a time in Scorsese's life rife with confusion and doubt. Yet, *After Hours* dropped *forty years ago*, and what I'm struck by is how one must live long enough for the re-boots and bridges to exist, i.e., one must possess the time, space, and life to figure out how to reinvent oneself when things are no longer working. Scorsese did, my father didn't, and here I am filled with grief and continually moving forward, as Scorsese did with *After Hours*.

- 1990 to 1999: **The Master Class, aka "I'm in Construction" stage,** followed by **2001-Present: The Busy Finale, aka "Sell Me This Pen!"**

We know the rest.

~

Is it the random vicissitudes of timing that "When I Paint My Masterpiece"—the Jerry Garcia Band version—is playing on shuffle in my Apple music library as I sit down to write this? I'll always associate the song with my father. Not that he ever mentioned it. I can't even say if he knew the song existed—he may have, it was written by Dylan, even if it was initially recorded by The Band (and let's note that Scorsese shot The Band's final performance, which resulted in the documentary *The Last Waltz*, widely regarded as a rock and roll masterpiece.)

I first heard "When I Paint My Masterpiece" in the early 1990s at a Grateful Dead show somewhere in Northern California, the message as I understood it in my stoner glory was that the protagonist's life—their artistic life anyway—had been challenging, and while they hadn't crafted a masterpiece yet, they would one day:

> *Yes, it sure has been a long hard climb*
> *Train wheels running through the back of my memory*
> *When I ran in the hilltop following a pack of wild geese*
> *Someday, everything is going to be smooth like a rhapsody*
> *When I paint my masterpiece.*

My father had to believe that this was true for him as well. Still, one works through their stuff—the stuck places—keeps creating, outlasts their children's needs, makes the time to create, finds their voice, their rhythm—and maybe then it happens. Perseverance is part of it. Grit as well. Being talented of course. Living long enough for all of it to coalesce. Scorsese at twenty-five seemed to have a head start on these things with *Who's That Knocking at My Door*, though as my father would've argued, *Raging Bull* is his masterpiece—unmatched before or since.

Is it important to note that in the early 1960s my father participated in the famous Washington Square Outdoor Art Exhibit in Greenwich Village when he was around the same age as Scorsese was when he directed *Who's That Knocking at My Door*, where he won first prize, and enjoyed an early taste of success? Or that my parents moved to Washington, DC, which led to a show at the Dixon Art Gallery in Georgetown, where even after my father sold out his entire show, they still moved to Binghamton, choosing to no longer live and create in the places where my father had found success and could have potentially built a greater career? Albert Boime had this to say about this period in my father's life: "[C]learly it was never a question of personal talent or skill, but a psychological disposition that drove him from competitive realms of activity. He needed to succeed on his own terms in a community that accepted him on his own terms."[11] This was Binghamton, which reminded my father of the Bronx, both in terms of its ethnic neighborhoods and working-class culture.

But is it also a coincidence that as "When I Paint My Masterpiece" comes on as I sit here, pen in hand, composition notebook open, a desire to capture the vibe I'm chasing with this work, *Killers of the Flower Moon* is dropping and saturating my news feeds? The artistic life and grief endlessly intertwined. I might pause here to say there's a method to the madness—my madness. Not that I consider what I'm attempting to do here madness. Still, I'll pause regardless. I intend to write the first draft of this book in real time. A swirling group of prompts and ideas gathered and listed that await my daily reaction, all of which have something to do with *After Hours*, Scorsese as artist, my father's artistic life and death, as well as the creation and nourishment of my own artistic life.

Which is to say, I want to capture the animated vibe of *The Basketball Diaries* by Jim Carroll and the autofiction meets journal flow of *Jacket Weather* by Mike DeCapite. They're both great New York authors and artists, the former a hero of mine since my teen years, the latter a more recent acquaintance. Other influences include Wendy C. Ortiz, Jackson Bliss, Ashley Marie Farmer, and Patti Smith, though what's important to capture here is how I'm trying to find my voice with this whole exercise and trying to paint my masterpiece— and like Scorsese, we're all products of the various inputs and impulses that govern our days and psyches.

So, is it coincidental then that "When I Paint Masterpiece" came on as I was planning to write or that it made its way onto these pages? Not at all, and not because it's fate or pre-ordained, but because everything is material and everything happens in real time—whatever is happening is happening, and not unlike *After Hours*, I'm trying to make sense of what's coming at me as I step into the *mostly* unknown. However, unlike Paul Hackett, I'm seeking to embrace the twists and turns of that unknown and let it ooze onto the pages before me.

INTERVIEW with Mike Decapite

Ben Tanzer: I'm here with Mike DeCapite. How are you?

Mike DeCapite: I'm good.

BT: When I was conceptualizing how I wanted to approach this book, *Jacket Weather* popped into my head. This whole idea of autofiction came up and I had this idea that I wanted this book to be like auto-nonfiction. I really wanted to write something every day in real time, not really plan it out, see what came up, and then write it like a journal entry. I have this memory of you talking about how *Jacket Weather* grew out of your journal entries.

MD: We think of things in the way that they're most helpful to us. When I was eighteen, I wrote a book of journals as a novel, or I wrote a novel as a book of journals, whatever. I typed them up every day and so it was bits of conversation and encounters and observations of the weather and whatever I wrote that day. I never did anything with that book, never tried to get it published. But that sort of became the template, that journalistic quality. Not journalistic, what's the word for it? The sort of quotidian quality of that. And the fragmentary quality of that became the template for whenever I tried to write a novel, since that's just kind of what I fall into, that's what comes naturally to me. So, that's how I wrote *Jacket Weather*. But I didn't write *Jacket Weather* as journals. There are fragments of it that came out of a little notebook that I wrote to June, my partner who the book is about…but I knew I was writing a novel.

BT: Your writing feels incredibly alive to me. And part of why

I love *Jacket Weather* and why I was sort of channeling it when I was thinking about my book was, "Mike's onto something with that energy. It's got that *The Basketball Diaries* thing; it feels like it's happening as I'm reading it."

MD: That's exactly what I wanted it to feel like. Another thing is that form, putting something together out of fragments and doing whatever you're going to do today, leaves you open to chance. And so, chance is part of the process. You know, it's not like when you sat down to write your list of ideas about your *After Hours* book. I'm sure there's a lot of stuff that winds up in there that you never would've thought of on the first day.

BT: Oh, absolutely.

MD: If something happens today, the phone rings and you have a funny conversation, you want to be able to stick that in the book. So that's another thing that hopefully helps it feel more alive and present. And then the other thing is that just when you're working on something, it puts you in the role of the observer…your alert in a way that you're normally not, or at least that I'm normally not. Usually I'm just trying to catch the train, or buy what I need before I go back upstairs, you know what I mean? This puts you in the role of the observer. You're always kind of thinking; you're always inside the book.

BT: Do you have any feelings about *The Basketball Diaries*?

MD: I remember liking the book a lot. However, it didn't open up a new world to me because I was already listening to the Velvet Underground, and I was reading William Burroughs, and I didn't come upon it when I was twelve like you did. I was already interested in that world and already wanted to move to New York. I just probably thought how lucky for this kid that he got to live this, that he got to live this experience and be authentically New York, which I was never going to be.

BT: What does New York mean to you now as a writer, as an adult? You wanted to get there. That to me, in a way, is the most New York thing there is. If you're not there, you want to be there.

MD: I feel like I can never leave New York because it's like a miracle that I'm here and that I've been here this long. And that in itself feels like an accomplishment. You know, to have to have spent this amount of time just getting by. I don't feel the kind of buzzing excitement about it all the time, like I have at other times in my life. It kind of wears off. Although New York is a place that you can always kind of just take one step back and look at symbolically in a way that I'm not sure happens in Cleveland. It has a currency. New York means something to everybody. It doesn't mean the same thing to everybody, but it means something. For a lot of people, New York is like the New York that they saw in *The Warriors*.

BT: I'm so glad you just mentioned *The Warriors*, it's one of the all-time great movies.

MD: That's one I haven't seen since it came out.

BT: It's genius, that doesn't mean it's good, just that it's genius. And not everyone I'm talking to has necessarily even seen *After Hours*, but you have associations with *After Hours*, which you saw in New York, correct?

MD: I saw it in a theater downtown. I want to say it was on Lafayette Street, one afternoon, and that I walked out of it into sort of a continuation of the movie. It's not like I lost my keys, but the city, and the setting was continuous with the movie. So, that's what I remember about it.

BT: Why do you think that was?

MD: Probably because I had just watched *Taxi Driver* and *Raging Bull* and other movies like *The Pope of Greenwich Village*. It was like six movies that we watched over and over again when those things were available on videotape.

~

What's happening now starts with a run. It often starts with a run. I put on the "WTF with Marc Maron Podcast" and listen to an interview he is doing with Warren Zanes, one-time member of the Del Fuegos and author of the new book, *Deliver Me From Nowhere: The Making of Bruce Springsteen's Nebraska*, an album I'm listening as I write this—the words of the title song bouncing around in my head, the tears forming as they always do when I hear these songs:

> *I can't say that I'm sorry*
> *For the things that we done*
> *At least for a little while, sir*
> *Me and her, we had us some fun.*

I might add here that one of my more obscure novels, *My Father's House*, a rumination on my father's death, is also an homage to the song with the same name from *Nebraska*:

I broke through the trees and there in the night
My father's house stood shining hard and bright
The branches and brambles tore my clothes and scratched my
arms
But I ran 'til I fell shaking in his arms

Does it make a difference that the father in Springsteen song can't be found? Or that Paul Hackett thought he would have some fun and instead ended up with torn clothes, scratched arms, and no one to save or embrace him—except June, briefly near the end of his journey (before she wrapped him in papier-mâché)? Or that "My Father's House" is framed as a dream—and what is *After Hours* if not the story of a man caught in a waking dream, who emerges from a place of isolation—where he's barely awake to his surroundings—into a dystopian urban nightmare, with no hope of solace or salvation?

Am I getting ahead of myself?

How would I know?

During the introductory monologue to his interview with Zanes, Maron talks about how it's the three-year anniversary of the death of his former partner, the director Lynn Shelton. Maron shares that he wasn't initially aware the anniversary was coming but felt that something was off. He went for a hike, and decided to listen to Taylor Swift because he didn't understand what she was all about. He put on her latest album, *Midnights*, and still didn't get it, until the song "Bigger Than the Whole Sky" came on—a song about death and grief. Then Maron knew exactly what he felt but had failed to identify.

Music and art can liberate what we prefer to bury and suppress as we seek to keep the sadness and turbulence at bay—a transaction which Scorsese and Springsteen, and yes, Taylor Swift get to be immersed and engaged in—and Shelton and my father don't. Whether that's fair or merely fucked-up isn't to be understood exactly, but it can be written about and filmed.

Maron shifts from his monologue to his conversation with Zanes, who himself has lived a life in art, nurturing it, creating it, living it. Zanes has gone from being a musician to an academic and a writer who's never quite stopped being a musician. He has stayed curious, thoughtful, reflective, pushing and bending his artistic life as far as it will go, including working with Scorsese on his acclaimed documentary *George Harrison: Living in the Material World.*

Here, Zanes has written about Springsteen, who having released *The River*—a true breakthrough album for him—and poised for super stardom, instead chose to write and record *Nebraska*, by himself, in a rented house. This was the culmination and manifestation of the depression, desolation, and darkness Springsteen felt at that stage of his life and career—pinned down by the trappings of success and unsure of his direction or what came next. Is this different from what Scorsese felt when he filmed *After Hours*? Yes and no. Both men despaired about the state of their art, though Scorsese faced a world with limited opportunities, while Springsteen's opportunities were unlimited. The resulting work in both cases, however, reflects who and where they were.

Does the best work emerge from such darkness? That's debatable. Springsteen followed *Nebraska* with *Born in the U.S.A.*, and Scorsese followed *After Hours* with *The Color of Money*, both massive hits. Zanes may or may not find massive success with his new book, and he may or may not care. Yet I was struck that Maron commented on how the book isn't a standard biography, but more a piece crafted distinctly in

Zanes' voice and a reflection of all he's done prior, absorbed, and been influenced by, not unlike the work I'm attempting to do here. Zanes comes at his book from multiple angles, and I'd be proud to think such a thing is possible for me with this book as well, finding a voice and crafting a story that embraces what's in my head and makes someone sing, tears and all.

~

Debbie is out of town and my younger son, Noah, is visiting my older son, Myles, at school. I've just returned from a poetry slam Noah co-hosted and performed in. After taking him to the Amtrak station, I chose to journal and write when I got home, over going for a run. I'd originally intended to do all three, but I went out for tacos and a margarita instead. I bought some Twizzlers on the walk home, mixed a generous gin & tonic once here, then fired-up *After Hours*.

Home alone, just as I'd been the first time I saw the film some thirty years ago. The circumstances are decidedly different, however. I'm not a teenager visiting from college and sitting in my parents' basement. I'm am also nearly thirteen years older than Scorsese was when *After Hours* came out. He was forty-two, which is to say I'm almost fifty-five.

Most of the movie is exactly as I remember it. The flow,

the performances, the dread and *tsuris*—described by *Moment* "as a Yiddish word...meaning trouble; its relative, litzrot, means narrow or to be in a tight place."[12] *After Hours* is about Paul Hackett (as Scorsese's stand-in) being in a tight place—a series of tight places really—and finally the tightest place, wrapped in papier-mâché, not unlike Munch's "The Scream"—a point made early in the movie when Paul meets Marcy's friend, the sculptress Kiki Bridges, played by the formidable Linda Fiorentino, who is working on a sculpture that echoes "The Scream." *After Hours* is tight and not singular. Paul may be confined to a single neighborhood, but he finds himself trapped by any number of people in any number of places and situations, though none more resistant to his escape than his own psyche—something I didn't totally grasp the first time I watched the movie.

From the start, Paul makes poor decisions and keeps making them. Technically, he can leave Soho whenever he wants—he just can't leave who and what he is. In the beginning a woman is the impetus for Paul's journey, Rosanna Arquette's Marcy. But she isn't the sole impetus any more than a single person is ever the impetus for the impulsive decisions we make in life.

One thing that strikes me watching the movie now is how

Paul is a creep in the early scenes, something I failed to register when I originally saw *After Hours*. Is this due to my age now versus then—John Hughes' movies didn't seem creepy then either, though it's hard to see them in any other way today. However, while Paul is a creep during his pursuit of Marcy, he's also lonely and isolated. How much does that factor into the story? A lot.

So, Paul is alone in a diner and responds to the slightest bit of attention from Marcy—who's nice, cute, and gives him her number. He returns home to his sad, empty apartment and, what he's not going to call her—no, of course he is.

When Paul arrives at the Soho apartment Marcy is staying in, the energy is off immediately. Kiki, who lives there, is aggressive and brusque and puts him to work on the papier-mâché sculpture. Marcy isn't there and when she calls the apartment it's clear she doesn't want Paul to be there either. Does it matter that Paul lost his twenty-dollar bill after it flew out of the cab window? It does in terms of his ability to easily get home. Yet, why does he stay and make a pass at Kiki while waiting for Marcy, or later make a pass at a clearly disinterested Marcy, before slipping out of the apartment when she isn't looking. Is everything that follows punishment for these actions?

Paul can't take the subway home because the fare goes up at midnight and he doesn't have enough money to pay for it. When he jumps the turnstile, an angry cop awaits him. Paul then heads to a bar where Tom, the bartender, played by John Heard, offers him subway fare if Paul can go to his apartment and retrieve the key to the cash register. Once there Paul encounters two burglars named Neil and Pepe—played by Cheech and Chong, respectively—who've apparently stolen Kiki's sculpture. We also learn that there's been a rash of unsolved burglaries in the neighborhood. The burglars drop the sculpture, and Paul decides to bring it back to Kiki. When he arrives at her apartment, Kiki insists that Paul apologize to Marcy for sneaking out. Does he have to? He chooses to do so and discovers that Marcy has committed suicide. In the interim, Kiki has left to go to a punk night club called Club Berlin with her boyfriend Horst. Paul returns to the bar where Tom works. It's closed. Paul sees a waitress—Julie, played by Terri Garr—who invites him to wait in her apartment across the street.

When Paul sees Tom return to the bar from Julie's window, he heads across the street and gives Tom the keys. Before Paul can get any money from Tom, howeverm Tom learns that his girlfriend Marcy has killed herself. Paul then returns to Julie's, and she makes a pass at him. Paul rejects her and heads to Club Berlin, where the bouncer will not let him enter under any circumstances—shades of *The Trial* by Kafka—but one; he must get a mohawk. Paul flees Club Berlin after sitting down for but not completing the mohawk. He then meets an ice cream truck driver played by Catherine O'Hara, who ultimately mistakes him for the person responsible for the burglaries in the neighborhood. She then joins an angry mob that chases Paul through Soho. Paul finds Tom again, to no avail. He then returns to Club Berlin, and dances with a sculptress named June—played by Verna Bloom—who covers him in papier-mâché to hide him from the mob but chooses not to remove the now hardened papier-mâché after the mob leaves. The burglars arrive and steal the hardened papier-mâché-covered Paul, placing him in the back of their van. Racing uptown through the New York streets, they take a sharp turn, and Paul falls out of the van, right in front of his office, where the papier-mâché breaks off. It's now morning, and Paul goes to work.

When I had my bachelor party in New York City in the mid-1990s, the night wasn't so far removed from *After Hours*. Following dinner at the iconic Lower East Side restaurant Sammy's Roumanian—monstrous steaks, bottles of vodka encased in ice, egg creams my father proudly made at the table, Leslie Nielsen and Philip Bosco dancing with dates—we moved on to Billy's Topless, where I decided to take a photo—not of a stripper, but a jukebox. The bouncer confiscated my camera as one of my friends screamed "fuck-off" at him and we were forcibly removed from the bar. On the way to Florent—where we'd eventually end-up—we stopped at a bar in the bowels of the meatpacking district, and among the vast, backlit aquariums filled with turtles casually swimming to and fro, the bartender, after learning I was getting married, grabbed me by my then long hair, yanked my head backwards onto the bar and poured tequila into my mouth from above. As the booze splashed across my face, the bar, and everything else, I was saved by someone screaming "Live Sex Show!" from somewhere in the back. We headed in that direction and found a room with a stage and rows of seats arranged theater style. On the stage was a man, handcuffed and blindfolded, as two female dominatrixes danced around and taunted him. As they began to undress him, the guy panicked, began to writhe, and tried to free himself, before tipping over in the chair and collapsing onto the stage. As he lay there, one of the dominatrixes asked, "does anyone want to get whipped?" My friend shouted yes. During the whipping, my father looked at me and asked, "how does this happen?" I replied, "you have to leave the house."

Which is all Paul Hackett wanted to do.

At one point, Paul goes home with a man who believes it's a hook-up. As Paul relays the events of his evening to this uncomfortable and disappointed stranger, the man asks him what he wants and Paul replies, "I want to live!"

Paul is scared he might be killed.

Scorsese was scared his career might be dead.

My father didn't want to die.

I don't either.

~

I want to live!

I write this after midnight, which means it's no longer May 31st, but June 1st, which also means I'm fifty-five years old. Which is fine. My age is only significant to me because I want to get to sixty. Well, I want to get beyond sixty, but sixty is a good start. Why? I've long felt sixty was the age when I could assess my life and question what I might want and be able to change.

Even in my twenties I felt like I needed to work, pursue a career, save money, hustle—head down, full time, full steam—and sixty felt like a reasonable time to ask, "what can be different now?" I felt at sixty I could become something different than I was. Whatever I was. I could work less. Read more. Go to the movies any time I wished. Eat more tacos. Drink more. A lot more. Maybe surf in the morning. Make movies. Something.

When Debbie and I had children in our thirties, after I'd just started to write, it became apparent to me that if things more or less developed as they should, Noah would finish college the year I turned sixty, and if I could have two children enter adulthood then, or be on the cusp of it anyway, change might really be possible. What kind of change? It wasn't clear, but it would involve living a more fully formed creative life. It's what being alive looked like to me.

It was about reimagining life.

My life.

If I'm fifty-five today, June 1st, this means my father's birthday looms as well, which was June 3rd. He would've been eighty-two. He's not. He died at fifty-nine. Fifty-nine. He didn't seem old then and he doesn't today. That's the other thing about turning sixty; it means I'll have outlived my father. It's not a competition, but it's the truth.

I want to live.

In *After Hours*, Paul Hackett fears for his life, though it's not the main concern of the movie—the main concern is that Paul Hackett doesn't feel alive.

He goes to the office, he goes home.

He tries to change things up and look at the results.

Still, does he feel alive that night?

He must have.

I don't need that.

Excitement.

Late night jaunts.

Dread.

There were times I did, and I pursued it.

Now, I'm good.

I want to be boring, normal.

I want to create.

I also want to be healthy, but control over that isn't always possible.

~

In 2002, when Scorsese was sixty, and my father was already dead, *Gangs of New York* was released, sandwiched between *Bringing Out the Dead* in 1999, a small Scorsese movie, nearly as terrific, weird, dread-ridden, and funny as *After Hours*, and

The Aviator in 2004, a clear event movie. These were followed by many more Scorsese movies, none of which my father got to see.

It's too easy to focus on how my father isn't here, which I do anyway, all the time, and the movies he's missing, and I'm not. There are numerous movies I associate with him being alive, which is important to me, because my father— and mother—lived life. (She still does.) They lived and loved large, driven by joy and pleasure. Traveling. Listening to music. Drinking coffee. Staying up late. These people were always up late—eating, talking, creating, and working, always working— and going to the movies. If not going to the movies, talking about movies.

One such movie I associate with my father is *Paris, Texas* by Wim Wenders. I don't recall why now and as I write this, I believe I sometimes confuse it with *Mystery Train* by Jim Jarmusch. They're from the same era, they're both indie, they share a vibe, and my father loved *Mystery Train*, so at times I must think they're the same movie.

I read last night that there was a special *Paris, Texas* screening scheduled for early today, the morning after I stayed up to watch *After Hours*. It seemed like kismet, and to attend the screening could even be a sort of tribute or homage to my father and the act of writing this book. I didn't make it. I stayed up to watch *After Hours*. Dozing off. Re-winding. Re-watching. It got late. I needed sleep. I also needed to get up and write, run, work, and read. Saturday stuff. Stuff that might have been rearranged if the timing of *Paris, Texas* had worked out. It didn't.

There's a path here that speaks to what a creative life might look like; it's an immersion in a kind of hanging out which intersects with a deep dive into art however and whenever it presents itself.

My father lived quite a bit like that when he lived.

Scorsese must as well.

I drift in and out of it, and my idea is to do less drifting in and out of it at some point. This involves peeling back from the work which pays the bills and following some other path, something akin to the artists' lives I aspire to and fantasize about, a path pertinent to this project—itself, an exercise in being alive so as to create an *After Hours* hagiography.

Hagiography, really?

Yes. Per *Merriam Webster*, a hagiography is (1) a biography of saints or venerated persons; or (2) idealizing or idolizing biography.

That works.

I write this even as Scorsese shared yesterday that he's interested in making another movie about Jesus and has met with the Pope, which also strikes me as a good time to note how little I've commented on *The Last Temptation of Christ*, the movie Scorsese couldn't get made before turning to *After Hours*. I've never seen it. Pause. I know. Still, the path here is this: *After Hours* as hagiography, seeking to understand the crafting and nurturing of a creative life through the lens of the movie, using my father's connection and attachment to the movie as a platform to grieve and celebrate his life and his art, a hagiography of sorts as well.

Which is to say, it's easy to overlook the more celebratory elements of life and movie watching as one grieves and hagiographisizes. And so, let me offer a list of movies I associate with my father—and in many cases my mother as well—which reflect his having lived a life that was full, creative, and coursed with love and pleasure, even if far from complete at the end:

1. *Paris, Texas*. Again, *Mystery Train* may be the more accurate selection here, but movies of a certain time and place, small, independent slices of America, nonmainstream, low cost, and authentic.

2. *Running on Empty.* I believe I saw it first with Debbie, and my father may not have even seen it, though I doubt that. No matter. What's important is the scene where Judd Hirsch sits in the living room, reading, late at night, as River Phoenix comes home, a few words at most shared between them, a nod maybe, more acknowledgement than anything. Yet love suffuses the scene, and that was my father and I during high school—him always up late reading, me walking in, a smile or look passed between us. This was who we were, if nothing else.

3. *The Warriors* and *Alien.* Both were released in 1979. My father took me to see them because I was a child and they were R-rated. They remain all-time greats for me, as formative as any movies I saw in childhood.

4. *Do the Right Thing.* My parents and I saw this the summer before my senior year in college. I was living in Albany, New York, and they came to visit. My father strongly encouraged me to watch *She's Gotta Have It*, which I did, on my VCR (I'd seen *School Daze* at the mall with my college friends, no encouragement required.)

They were both something. However, *Do the Right Thing* was something else entirely. And still is. It was *Raging Bull*.

5. *Caddyshack*. My father loved this movie and Rodney Dangerfield, specifically. No more so than when his character, Al Czervik, yells during the closing moments of the film, "Hey everybody! We're all gonna get laid!"—a line ScreenRant believes to be one of twenty best in film history.[13]

6. *A Bronx Tale*. This is included because my father was from the Bronx, grew up during the era depicted in the film, and didn't feel it was realistic or true to the world he knew. While I don't recall him complaining about many movies, this one didn't sit well with him. He didn't talk much about this childhood, though as time has passed, I'm not sure if this was because it wasn't an easy one, or because I didn't ask. Unlike the father-son dynamic in *Frequency*, the answer is lost to history.

7. *Raging Bull*. The brother dynamics, New York City, the violence, pain, and isolation. It was all there, shot

beautifully in black and white. My father considered it a masterpiece, and yet it somehow lost the Oscar to *Ordinary People*, which my father considered tragic.

8. *La Cage Aux Folles*. We saw this in Provincetown, possibly my parents' favorite place in the world, the summer when I was ten years old, and my brother was eight. My mother asked the woman at the ticket booth if she thought the movie was appropriate for children— please note this was Provincetown during the summer of 1978. She shrugged and said, "I think so," and my parents bought the tickets. My dad always loved that exchange. What else was she going to say?

9. *The Match Factory Girl*. My father, mother, Debbie, and I saw this at the Film Forum in New York City in 1990. *The Los Angeles Times* described it as a "weirdo masterpiece, to be sure." Debbie and I found it more akin to low-grade psychological torture. *The Match Factory Girl* is bleak and slow, and while it may require a re-watch, *Repo Man* in comparison, always felt like an actual "weirdo masterpiece" to me. *The Match Factory Girl* is no *Repo Man*.

10. *Hard Eight.* My father encouraged me to see this when few of us had any idea who Paul Thomas Anderson was, and as far as I'm concerned, my father discovered Paul Thomas Anderson. Care to disagree?

These are my associations. I texted my mother while thinking about this and I asked her what she thought my father's favorite movies were. She wrote, "*Seventh Seal,* Bergman, all the Kurosawa movies, particularly *Rashomon. Five Easy Pieces, Easy Rider.*" This tracks for me. He talked about these movies, though I needed my mother to both remind me of this and validate it. I also asked her what her favorites were. I wanted to know, and as noted, I don't write about her enough. She sent me a lengthy text which concluded with, "A conversation about the films would be easier for me."

Okay.

INTERVIEW with Judy Tanzer

Ben Tanzer: Please introduce who you are, what you do, and how I know you.

Judy Tanzer: Judy Tanzer. I am Ben's mother, a retired psycho-therapist, and an avid moviegoer.

BT: I was interested in having you participate in this for many reasons, but one of them is that I always saw our family as one that looked at our relationship through the lens of what movies we saw. How do you see the importance of movies to yourself, but also to our family as a unit?

JT: I started going to the movies when I was probably six or seven. I went regularly, both with friends, by myself, and then obviously with my husband, your father, and then with the whole family. But I never framed it as a kind of indicator of where my life was, until you said it to me. Then I realized that it must be true. You know, we always went to the movies on Friday nights, because after we worked, I always wanted to go. I wanted to get lost at the movies. It was like somewhere else. Someplace else. I really left my world and went into that world. I do the same thing now. If I get immersed in something, it's like everything else goes away. And then I'm in that world of whatever. And there's no more perfect place to be in another world than in the movies.

When I was young, in the 1950s, there were all those

Hollywood movies. I don't think I identified with them particularly. The first time I saw a movie that wasn't a mainstream Hollywood movie was in Baltimore when I was sixteen, which was *Hill 24 Doesn't Answer*, which was an Israeli film. Then I went to see another art house film. Then I saw an English movie. And those were the first non-mainstream Hollywood movies I ever saw.

In my second year at the University of Chicago, which would've been 1959, I saw an Ingmar Bergman movie, *The Virgin Spring*. I had never heard of Bergman before. I went to see it by myself, it was kind of a scary movie...but it changed everything. I wasn't conscious of that at the time, I didn't say, "oh, this changes everything." But from then on, and because of the way the 1960s were with movies, there was this tremendous influx of foreign films.

Then I moved to New York and went to the movies all the time. On the first or the second date with Mike, my husband, your father, I went to see *Jules and Jim*. I remember that specifically because I was thinking about whether Mike was going to call me. I came home and he called that night, and we went to see the movie. And then he and I went to the movies all the time. I always had a favorite film. First it was *The Taste of Honey*, then it was *La Strada*, which is almost my all-time favorite movie. And then I saw *Amarcord*, which I think is my all-time favorite.

Then we were living in Binghamton. We were starved for movies there, since there weren't any non-mainstream theaters. So we went to Provincetown, where there were two theaters that showed non-mainstream movies. That was in the 1970s. Mike and I would travel to places to see films. I read a review of a Japanese movie called *In the Realm of Desire*. It was written about as a political film, but it was completely erotic. I read that the movie was playing in New York, so I went. I used to go to New York a lot anyway, but I went to the city on like a Friday or Saturday afternoon to see the film. There were like four people in the theater. I think it was in the Paris Theater, which is near 59th and Columbus Circle. I was the only woman. The film was so erotic. It was about oral sex. The ecstasy of it. It kept repeating. But it's like with sex, at some point it's great, and then you get tired of it.

BT: I've heard that, yes.

JT: So that's what happened. By the end of the movie, I was like, okay, I've seen enough oral sex to last for a lifetime. It was a very funny experience because I thought, God, I'm the only woman in this theater. But it remained one of those special sorts of experiences. I've got so many stories. I mean, it's unbelievable. But given one of the primary focuses of this book, I think what's interesting is that I've always been so immersed in Martin Scorsese.

BT: Could you talk about the importance of Scorsese to you, and by extension Dad, and what his movies have meant to you.

JT: Scorsese, how do I want to put it? I mean, as a director, the first movie we saw of his was *Mean Streets.* We followed Scorsese, we read about him, or at least I read about him, and we discussed him a lot. We thought he was the best American director that we had ever seen. That's what I guess was significant. Before Scorsese, it was really all the European directors and the Japanese and the Indians and the Russians. American movies were not something that we saw a lot. Then Scorsese comes along, and it changes. And of course, *Mean Streets* is New York, right? It's the Lower East Side. Dad, of course, was a New Yorker. He knew that neighborhood, Mulberry Street, Little Italy. I had never lived there. But we were living close to there then. We lived near the Village, and then we lived in Brooklyn. So, for Dad, the people in *Mean*

Streets and the later films, he could probably associate them more because he grew up in New York. The streets of New York were his world.

BT: What are your feelings about *After Hours*?

JT: What I remember is how I felt. I went to see the movie at the Oakdale Mall on a Saturday afternoon. It was probably raining, it was Binghamton, so it was at least overcast. I'm sort of in a depressed state. I was probably the only person in the theater. And the movie was so depressing to me. I thought, why in the hell did I go to see this movie? But I didn't leave; it was compelling enough for me to stay. What I remember is the darkness of the film. And of course, I was in the dark theater, and I was in a dark place. So, when I left the movie, I was really depressed. I want to use a more particular word for it. I think the word is despair.

~

One thing I can't talk about with my mother is Martin Scorsese's favorite movies. Luckily, I don't need Mom for this as I have an Indiewire article from May 2023 titled "Martin Scorsese's Favorite Movies: 70 Films the Director Wants You to See."[14]

1. *Ikiru* by Akira Kurosawa (1952). This film is about a man searching for meaning at the end of his life—and at the end of his life, I'm certain my father could have related. Among other things, he wondered whether he should've abandoned Judaism, and if not doing so might have saved his life.

2. *Tár* by Todd Field (2022). This is a far more recent film by the director of one of my all-time favorite movies, *In the Bedroom*. I was struck by Scorsese's comments about the film at the New York Film Critics Circle awards, where he suggested that too many films today take us by the hand and let us know where they're going—not Tár: "The world is her. Time, chronology and space, become the music that she lives by. And we don't know where the film's going. We just follow the character on her strange, upsetting road to her even stranger final destination." (So, we have Kafka's work, *After Hours*, and now *Tár*, all involving dislocation, fear, and the sense that we don't know where we're going or what comes next.)

3. *Pearl* by Ti West (2022). Scorsese loves this movie as

does my son, Myles. As Scorsese says about *Pearl*, "Ti West's movies have a kind of energy that is so rare these days, powered by a pure, undiluted love for cinema. You feel it in every frame." Why else watch movies?

4. *The Shining* by Stanley Kubrick (1980). Scorsese has a thing for horror movies, including this one, which I also watched in my parents' basement back when it was first released. Scorsese, who didn't read the book as I did, calls it "a majestically terrifying movie where what we don't see or comprehend shadows every move the characters make." (Shades of *After Hours*, which may not be terrifying, at least not to me, but is about not being able to comprehend what we're seeing or why anyone—especially, though not only Paul Hackett—is doing what they're doing.)

While I don't associate horror movies with my father, Myles loves them, and I watched *The Shining* with him. I did so with trepidation, however—what if he didn't like it? Which is also a thing. We may want to bequeath a love of cinema to our children, but we also want our children to love the movies we love. For example, I watched *Easy Rider* in my parents' basement one night, knowing my father loved it, but

I didn't get it. When our children don't love what we love, it can be heartbreaking. That wasn't the case here, as Myles— and Noah—love *The Shining*. Not that either of them found it scary.

Spike Lee is on Scorsese's list with *BlaKkKlansman*, but there's no Paul Thomas Anderson, Brian DePalma or Jim Jarmusch. No Barry Jenkins. There's Francis Ford Coppola, but no Sofia Coppola, or Greta Gerwig. Or Noah Baumbach. No Jordan Peele. *The Public Enemy* didn't make the list, which I expected it to, as my father talked about that movie all the time. There's also *A Trip to the Moon*, a 1902 short film which was featured in Scorsese's 2011 movie, *Hugo*, which I got Myles to watch with me in an actual theater. Also, *The Ten Commandments*, a movie I associate with being on late at night when I was a child. Scorsese had the following to say about it: "DeMille presented a fantasy, dream-like quality on film that was so real, if you saw his movies as a child, they stuck with you for life."

Scorsese also includes *East of Eden* and *Rebel Without a Cause* on his list, both of which have James Dean in common, an actor my father spoke about with a kind of reverence. And why wouldn't he? Dean was cool and real and seething with pain. While my father's response to Dean wasn't unique, his reaction certainly spoke to me.

~

Because coolness is a thing, right? And Scorsese knows this, having worked with some of the coolest actors and actresses around. Robert De Niro. Jack Nicholson. Leo DiCaprio. Margot Robbie. Daniel Day Lewis. Cate Blanchett. Linda Fiorentino. Harvey Keitel. Willem Dafoe. Ray Liotta. Juliette Lewis. John C. Reilly. Kevin Corrigan. And on and on.

Scorsese also understands that violence is cool at its most visceral and textual level, and those who know how to wield it—see Lewis in *Gangs of New York*, De Niro in *Cape Fear*, Pesci in *Goodfellas*—possess a coolness we revere, until we don't—see Lewis in *Gangs of New York*, De Niro in *Cape Fear*, Pesci in *Goodfellas*.

This raises the question of not only what's cool, but what's cool to you or me, the beholder. Michael Jordan may be a petty dude, but he's cool as hell. David Bowie was fucking cool, period. Ditto Riz Ahmed. Chloe Sevigny. Michaela Cole. Keith Haring. Harry Dean Stanton. Serena Williams. Spike Jonez. Ike Reilly. Thomas Campbell. Eve Babitz. Raymond Pettibon. Christy Turlington. Joey Ramone. Jean-Michel Basquiat. Justin Torres. Tony Fitzpatrick. Jay-Z and Beyonce.

Ed Ruscha. Adam Horovitz—with props to all the Beasties. Virgil Abloh. Takashi Murakami. They transcend. They back it up. They go about their business.

Also, cool: punk music, and the tune, "People who Died."

Poetry.

New York City in its bountiful, grimy wonder.

Jim Carroll, who for me is as quintessential New York as anyone.

Besides Scorsese of course.

And my dad, at one time.

~

Debbie and I watch what may be the last episode of *Ted Lasso*—a one-time critical and popular darling and now more of a conduit for channeling hate, frustration, and disappointment. This final iteration of the show and what it's perceived to have evolved into—preachy and too positive— doesn't bother me. It's a show that wanted to be about kindness and giving oneself grace in the face of grief and childhood trauma. Much of the grief revolves around failed relationships, poor communication skills, lack of self-awareness, shit, and/ or dead fathers. My father wasn't shit, but he is dead—and it's worth noting that I write this just two days removed from what would have been his eighty-second birthday. Not that he came close to making it to that birthday, and not that death means one can't pause on that person's birthday and wonder what things might have looked like if they had lived.

Scorsese's father, Charles, lived until eighty and is identified as an actor, should one look him up online. His credits start with *Taxi Driver* and include everything from *The Color of Money* to *Goodfellas* and *After Hours*.

My father would have been happy with such opportunities.

For good measure, Robert De Niro's father, Robert De Niro Sr., was an abstract expressionist painter from Syracuse, New York, who studied at Black Mountain College under Josef Albers and then with Hans Hoffman at his Provincetown summer school. De Niro Sr. later moved to a loft in Greenwich Village with his fellow student Virginia Admiral, where they surrounded themselves with friends such as Anais Nin, Henry Miller, and Tennessee Williams. De Niro Sr. would go on to create and exhibit work to great acclaim—and that work can still be found in the permanent collections of the Hirshhorn Museum and Sculpture Garden, the Metropolitan Museum of Art, the Whitney Museum of American Art, and many others. He would die at seventy-one of what else, cancer, in New York City. De Niro Sr. had the kind of career my father wanted; they even look somewhat alike—and it's impossible not to wonder, what if?

For what it's worth, Griffin Dunne, also born in New York City, is the son of Dominick Dunne, who produced both *The Boys in the Band* and *The Panic in Needle Park*—a movie my father endlessly referenced in part because it starred a young Al Pacino in his first lead role. Griffin Dunne is also the nephew of the authors John Gregory Dunne—Dominick's his older brother—and Joan Didion, the latter of whom needs little introduction and could certainly be added to my list of cool.

All of this is to say that our father's shadows loom large, and much of Ted Lasso's life is overshadowed by his father's suicide, which is at least in part responsible for Lasso's near toxic mix of positivity and kindness. Despite the animosity directed towards the final season of the show, and the very human desire to destroy that which we love, or once loved too much, the show was a welcome salve for many of us during the heights of the pandemic.

As is my predilection, I sought out recaps of the final episode of *Ted Lasso*, and as I read the *New York Times* take, I stumbled into an article published on my father's birthday (June 3, 2023) titled, "10 Movies That Capture the Essence of New York."[15] The article opens with a question: "What makes for a strong New York movie?" It goes on to answer that question with the following: "The standouts are often, like the city itself, unpredictable, a little shabby around the edges, sometimes exasperating but always compelling."

Okay, I feel that.

The article goes on to talk about the upcoming Tribeca Film Festival, and how the festival has always been a fan of such movies, and how this year it'll feature *A Bronx Tale*, Robert De Niro's directorial debut. The article adds: "The film shows a reverence for the neighborhood in which much of it takes place, and Mr. De Niro brings a knowing eye to the material."

My father would disagree.

Other films on the list include:

Taxi Driver. My parents simply loved this movie, a "nightmare story by Paul Schrader that makes the city pulse with an irresistible vibrancy and vigor."[16]

In the Heights. I'm not sure many people saw this movie, but it was the first film that Myles and I saw in a theater during the pandemic. Is it "as alive as it is poignant?" Maybe. Is it alive and glorious? Absolutely.

Dog Day Afternoon. I first saw this as part of an adult film class focused on New York movies that I took in the early 1990s. I was breathless watching it, and it was also another favorite of my parents. As the *Times* article says, "The city can certainly be a place to find spectacle." Also, there's Al Pacino, unhinged and overacting in the best of ways.

Do the Right Thing. A favorite, a masterpiece, and "a love letter to the richness and brashness of personality this city holds."

Being John Malkovich. I don't think of this as a New York City movie, though I don't think of *Die Hard* as a Christmas movie either. I just know I love them both.

After Hours. Of course, and yes, it's "kinetic," as described in the article, but there's also this: "Anyone who has stayed out late enough in New York to know how weird things can get should be able to relate."

I can relate, and when I go on to punch the phrase "New York movies" into Google, I discover a *Condé Nast Traveler* article from May 2020 titled "49 Movies That Will Transport You to New York City," with the subtitle, "Hope you like rom-coms and Martin Scorsese."[17] There are a few surprises here, *Ghostbusters* for example, which I suppose is a New York City movie, but there's also *After Hours*, again, and this, "The series of unfortunate events he encounters are simultaneously weird, morbid, and slapstick-funny—in other words, a perfect representation of New York's 1980s punk art scene."

"1980s punk art scene."

When did Jim Carroll's "People Who Died" come out? 1980.

Refracted through the lens of who or what may be the most punk anything and the most New York City anything, the answer isn't Carroll—not when the Ramones exist. Similarly, Scorsese is not unquestionably the most cineastic the city has to offer—Spike Lee, Noah Baumbach, and yes, Woody Allen, are all in the running. However, Jim Carroll and *The Basketball Diaries* play a quintessential role in my New York City, just as *After Hours* reflects the version of the city that appeals most to me. The overlap is punk and a New York that is raucous and without rules—even if the stories themselves are otherwise dissimilar.

When the team behind *Ted Lasso* wanted to do a one-off,

or bottle, episode of the show during season two, they chose to focus on a depressed Coach Beard going off on a late-night adventure in Amsterdam—a night filled with confusion, the threat of violence, and dislocation. The title of the episode? "Beard After Hours." As the *New York Times* wrote in a recap of the episode, "Now if you wanted to film a stand-alone episode with virtually no connection to what came before or after, *After Hours* is a fairly intuitive choice for inspiration."[18] (Please note that the author of the article enjoyed neither the episode nor *After Hours*.)

On the same day I allowed myself to disappear down the *Ted Lasso* rabbit hole, a clip emerged from the reality show, *The Family Stallone*, which stars among other family members, Sylvester himself. In this clip, he is having pizza with Al Pacino. They talk about why Sly is doing the show, to which he replies that he has a "cool" personality, so why not show it off? Pacino answers that, "everything happens if you stay alive." To which Stallone responds, "Yeah, you gotta point there."

Yeah, he does—you just have to stay alive.

Jim Carroll died at sixty. He had a heart attack. He was ill with pneumonia and hepatitis C. He was at his desk, working.

~

Teddy sniffing glue he was twelve years old
Fell from the roof on East Two-nine
Cathy was eleven when she pulled the plug
On twenty-six reds and a bottle of wine
Bobby got leukemia, fourteen years old
… They were all my friends and just died.

And so on.

I'm not certain there's anything super deep going on in "People Who Died," though a post on the site Musician Wages titled, "The Meaning Behind The Song: *People Who Died* by Jim Carroll Band," offers this: "By listing their names and the causes of their deaths, Carroll captures a sense of both celebration and mourning. This song is a powerful tribute to those who have departed, ensuring that their memories live on through the music."[19]

The song is all that—joyous, sort of punk, and a reminder that we may keep people alive through art, but we need to stay alive to make that art. Scorsese is as much an example of both things as anybody. Maybe when he decided to make *After Hours*, he wasn't certain this would remain the case. That merely staying alive was not going to be enough. And maybe every time he completes a project he wonders: will this be it?

Still, he must stay alive to make the next one, and the public must care enough to see what he creates.

Did the public care about Jim Carroll's work?

I don't know.

I did.

Adam Lawrence did, too. Adam being the friend who first introduced me to *The Basketball Diaries* at the age of twelve. Adam, who also introduced me to the Ramones and *The Rocky Horror Picture Show*. Adam, who got us tickets to see Bruce Springsteen on the *Born in the U.S.A.* tour.

Adam is important.

I only occasionally meet people beside Adam and I who've read *The Basketball Diaries*. Many more seem to have seen the movie. Those who've read the book tend to love it. I gave it to Noah to read, then held my breath.

He loved it, too.

I wrote about the book several years ago for the "Writers Recommend" column at "TNBBC's The Next Best Book Blog." I tried to sum up my feelings about a book I had read and re-read repeatedly between the ages of twelve and eighteen:

It was electric, and real time, all live wire, and nerve

endings, a mash-up of masturbation, drugs, sports, underage sex, predators, crime, writing, hustle, art, New York City in the mid-sixties, and people love to talk about cities, especially New York City as characters in stories, but usually they don't know what the fuck they're talking about, here though New York City was oozing and fresh, and another breathing slice of a book, that was so graphic, vivid, and fraught with gunk and stickiness, it was like watching a documentary.

Then I added this:

And then there is the language, fluid, poetic and crass, a twisty mix of slang and detail, all piling-up on itself, until it becomes something more than language, something visual, a fever dream, or overture, filled with spiky notes, and jazz beats.[20]

I imagine it would've been impossible not to be taken with all this when I was twelve and first got the book from Adam, but looking back I must've wondered if this was what the future could hold—girls and sports and grit and hustle and living in New York City.

"Jim Carroll was real, he was punk, and he was legend."

I wrote that, too.

For the post, I also re-read the book for the first time in years to see if it still spoke to me. I'd forgotten much of the second half, which is rife with shooting junk and nodding out at Riker's Island, and how some of it is draggy and repetitive, though also sad and funny. Overall, the book remained brilliant and beautiful and as lyrical as it ever was.

It also happens that in the early 1990s when I lived in New York City, Adam Lawrence called me at work one day and said, "Hey, meet me at The Bottom Line tonight, Jim Carroll is performing." Carroll wasn't even the headliner, Allen Ginsberg was—yes, that Allen Ginsberg, who just before Jim Carroll went on walked up behind where I was sitting and put his hands on my shoulders to get a better look at the stage.

How was Jim Carroll? He was gaunt and loose-limbed, vibrating, and stalking the stage like the punk, junkie, spider he was—a God in all his glory. All he had to do was leave my apartment and show up, and I was electrified. Isn't that the urgent pull illustrated by *After Hours* as well—Paul Hackett must leave his apartment to see what's possible.

I saw Jim Carroll one more time after that. It was in

Chicago. I was by myself, the room nearly empty. Carroll read the same piece he'd read at The Bottom Line. He wasn't loose-limbed and vibrant anymore; instead, he was tentative, and felt stuck in place, no longer raw nerves and energy, a shell of what he'd once been.

It was a reminder of the other pull in *After Hours*—that we must be alive and engaged for anything to happen.

~

There's something else about *The Basketball Diaries*, something I didn't recall until I re-read it—Jim Carroll writes in the book about becoming an actual author:

> The more I read the more I know it now, heavier each day, that I need to write. I think of poetry and how I see it as just a raw block of stone ready to be shaped, that way words are never a horrible limit to me, just tools to shape. I just get the images from the upstairs vault (it all comes in images) and fling 'em around like bricks, sometimes clean and smooth and then sloppy and ready to fall on top of you later.

It's impossible to read this now and not believe something

was put in motion for me when I read it for the first time.

Would I be a writer without *The Basketball Diaries* or Jim Carroll?

Would this book exist?

Several years ago, I decided that the next time I signed a book contract, I would have some piece of that long quote from Carroll inked onto my arm—both as tribute and homage. When I signed the contract for this book—on my birthday—I got a tattoo that read: "words are never a horrible limit to me."

And they haven't been.

INTERVIEW with Adam Lawrence

Ben Tanzer: Hello, Adam Lawrence. How are you?

Adam Lawrence: Hello, Ben Tanzer. I'm fine, thank you.

BT: Can you share how we know each other?

AL: I would date it to our meeting in second grade in the hallways of MacArthur Elementary School, when we were both in detention.

BT: I'm interested in talking to you partially because we go way back, but because I also consider you to be one of the most profound influences on my interests and obsessions. You introduced me to The Ramones and *The Basketball Diaries*, for example. You have also lived in New York City for a long time, and I want to know what the city means and has meant to you?

AL: My great-grandmother lived in a really nice building in the West Village, and *The Basketball Diaries* painted a picture of a New York that I didn't know much about, as far as what the city was, and its energy was, and how much different it was from a place like Binghamton, where we grew up.

BT: I don't think I ever really thought of *The Basketball Diaries* as New York City when we were kids because it almost seemed like a fairytale, obviously the darkest fairytale possible. When did you feel like you wanted to get out of Binghamton, and was New York City where you wanted to be?

AL: By junior high, if I had any goals or aspirations at all, it was that I would work in comics, which got me interested in art. In my head I was like, "if I'm going to be working in comics, I have to be in New York." That's where Marvel is, that's where DC is.

BT: Which leads me to *After Hours*. I don't know if it's the most New York movie, but it's certainly the most something.

AL: It's certainly the most, you've left your apartment, or you've left your job, and you have a sort of plan, but you don't. And then the universe and everything else in the city and all of that just absolutely takes over if you let it. Or you can't stop it. And those are kind of amazing, magical, thrilling, sometimes scary, sometimes mundane, times. All of that kind of feels like New York.

BT: When I saw you several months ago in New York City, I mentioned that I was going to pester you for an interview about *After Hours*, and you said that you had just gone to an anniversary showing of the movie.

AL: Yes, I saw it at the Paris Theater, which is an older movie theater that Netflix recently purchased. It was a 35-millimeter screening. It was the first time that I saw the movie projected on a screen, which was super cool.

BT: What was it like watching it again?

AL: It hadn't been so desperately long that it was like mind blowing in that way. It was more like you might not remember the order of the scenes, or there are a couple of scenes that you forgot or remember differently. But it's just always so satisfying to watch it again. And it really does keep hitting that same vibe, if that makes any sense. It really is a movie that hasn't transformed badly over the years as much as other films. It's still so much itself, and it's still so relatable.

~

Does it say something about me, this project, or my writing career, such as it is, that I couldn't carve out the time to write yesterday? That I had to teach in the morning. That I wanted to get some sleep, in preparation for my evening plans, Dead & Company and getting some afternoon drinks, so I didn't get up early to write. Or while I might've had time after my morning class to write, I didn't want to mess with my afternoon plans either, because pre-show drinking and shooting pool with my longtime friend and one-time New York City partner in crime, Avi, felt more important than making time for writing.

How does it work when there are other things going on which I want or need to attend to?

I could've written right after class and then shot pool, but it would've messed up my plans.

It would've been selfish.

I've been selfish with my time.

All the time.

How can't I be?

I missed yesterday, and I've missed other days over the years, many days—too many?

What if I hadn't missed those days?

Might I be more successful?

Had a greater impact?

Would I have more options, and if not more adulation, more of an artistic life?

What if I never missed a day of writing?

The thing is bills must be paid.

Retirement and college savings must be put away.

Children must be parented, loved, and listened to.

Wives and mothers must be treated with the gratitude and respect they deserve.

Sleep and Dead shows must happen as well.

And shooting pool?

Yes, in general.

With Avi?

Definitely.

Pool was my father's game, what he did when he skipped school, before he dropped out. I wanted to find a way to be with my father, and pool seemed like the space where we could make this happen, and we did, in Binghamton, Manhattan, Syracuse and Albany, Baltimore, Chicago—wherever we were.

This extends to Avi as well.

We shoot, we always have, we always will.

Which means I don't write.

~

One topic my father wanted to discuss while shooting stick was how "it" worked. "It" being the building of a successful career for himself—more sales, gallery and museum shows, permanent collections, notoriety. I couldn't answer that—though I didn't think his living in Binghamton helped. One must schmooze and network where the people are who can open doors, showcase your work, and further your career.

One must be in places like New York, Chicago, and Los Angeles.

One must be out there and alive in it.

I've done some of it myself, the hustle, pitching, making connections, yet I don't live like my father did. I'm not all art, all the time.

I had never truly contemplated what might be required of me until I read *Just Kids* by Patti Smith. If *After Hours* is a homage and celebration of the art scene that was downtown NYC, Patti Smith is the godmother of that scene, as well as the poet laureate of all things New York City punk. She escaped from New Jersey, landed in New York in the late 1960s, and over the next decade plus would form a relationship with the photographer Robert Mapplethorpe, live in the Chelsea Hotel, perform at CBGB's, and release her acclaimed debut album *Horses*. Smith would also interact with countless downtown figures, including Jim Carroll, who she would describe in *Just Kids* as "...unreliable, evasive and sometimes too stoned to speak, but he was also kind, ingenuous, and a true poet. I knew he didn't love me, but I adored him anyway. Eventually he just drifted away, leaving me a long lock of his red-gold hair." Smith would also appear in what else, a Scorsese film, the documentary *Rolling Thunder Revue* about Bob Dylan's 1975 tour of the same name.

What lingers about *Just Kids* for me is what Smith and

Mapplethorpe, and numerous others before and since, were willing to endure to make art. They were hungry. Lacking money and shelter. Or any sign that greatness awaited them beyond their belief that greatness awaited them.

I've never lived like that, the closest possibly being when I lived in New York City and worked as a case worker, living paycheck to paycheck and counting pennies at the end of the month—but still there was a regular paycheck, health insurance, a roof over my head, and a girlfriend who made more than me and paid half of everything.

I didn't write then. I wanted to but could never have fathomed living like Smith or Mapplethorpe, or even Adam Lawrence, who worked in independent films.

Is it required, living like that? *Just Kids* doesn't argue against it, though the book is a reminder that seeking kindred spirits who'll push you, love you, support you, and make you believe you must create based on the mere fact they believe in you goes a good way towards achieving any kind of success or finding any kind of voice. It's not everything, just as being born or living in New York City isn't a requirement, either. It just doesn't hurt.

~

What makes Scorsese great?

Arguably, his body of work is a manifestation of greatness. But what enables it? A 2022 article titled, "Martin Scorsese: 5 Things That Make Him Great,"[21] asked this question.

What are the five answers?

First, Scorsese has a "genuine interest in the stories he tells," and topics he loves, including crime and violence, the search for the meaning of life, as well as an interest in music and film, the latter of which is most clearly illustrated by the documentaries he makes.

Second, he knows his craft. Scorsese surrounds himself with the finest collaborators and has championed actors who've gone on to become stars after appearing in his movies.

Third, he refuses to be put in a box. Scorsese may be "a chronicler of violent American society," but he's also directed notable black comedies, such as *After Hours*.

Fourth, he knows film history: "Scorsese builds on American, European and Asian cinema traditions."

Fifth, he works tirelessly. So, despite the love and care Scorsese brought to *The Color of Money*, he probably doesn't take the afternoon off to shoot pool and drink.

~

I want to know why Scorsese wanted to make movies. I know that he was a frail and sickly child whose parents wouldn't let him play sports and took him to the movies instead. I also know he considered becoming a priest, though he went to NYU Film School. I suppose what I really want to know is, when did he know? At what point could he no longer not think about becoming a filmmaker? Did he wake up one morning and realize—as I once did—that something wasn't working, that he should be happier, that things could be better?

I can't ask my father if such a moment existed for him.

Nor Jim Carroll.

When I had that moment twenty-five years ago, I knew I'd have to start writing. It was the only viable option going forward. Plus, I'd already been thinking about it for years.

How long had I been thinking about it?

It started at the end of high school in 1986 and the creative writing class I was required to take and ended up loving, with its obligatory daily journaling and prompts. It continued through college—and the one creative writing class I took there, where there was no journaling, no prompts, just workshopping stories with horrible people—and graduation in 1990. Then onto and into my life in San Francisco.

I wrote my first post-college journal entry on January 11th, 1992, quoting my long-time friend Pete, who said of my life in the Bay Area, "At least you're killing time in a pseudo-productive way."

I never saw living there, and that life, as killing time, though that life—though not all of it—was much like Paul Hackett's. I worked in an office from nine to five. I sat at a desk in front of a computer. I rarely had to leave my seat. I arrived on time and wasn't expected or encouraged to work late. I had to bill for 7.25 hours per day and there were limits on how much time I could bill for tasks such as xeroxing. I didn't have nights like Paul Hackett's—well, not ones which felt dangerous—until I moved to New York City.

However, the San Francisco I lived in from 1990 to 1992 wasn't bleak or isolating. It was alive. People were forever out and about. It was pre-dotcom, and the rent was still cheap. Everyone seemed to be creating something. Or talking about it. Not that I was.

I went to work.

I also got high, dropped acid, consumed mushrooms, took Ecstasy, and tried something called Euphoria.

I played ultimate frisbee.

I ate Mission burritos.

I went to bars, clubs, and raves.

I attended Dead shows.

I hiked and hugged Redwoods.

I saw a lot of movies.

I didn't watch television outside of professional football and March Madness.

I was in the world.

Something was missing though, and I started to go to coffee shops to journal. I also started reading deeper and more philosophical books. I became a searcher, and these books reinforced whatever had been happening to me as I headed west in the first place. I found myself quoting the books I read on the pages of my journal. For example, from *The Teachings of Don Juan: A Yacqui Way of Knowledge*:

> ...a path without a heart is never enjoyable. You have to work hard even to take it. On the other hand, a path with heart is easy, it doesn't make you work at liking it.

These sentences spoke to me at the time, and I believe they could've spoken to Paul Hackett as well. Reading them, he might've recognized he was missing something, too. Paul is alone, he's trapped and searching for a spark. A way to be alive.

Does Paul want more, though?

I don't know.

I know I did.

~

The book, *My Father's List*, came to my attention after the author Laura Carney pitched herself for an interview on my podcast. I'd already been aware of Carney from following her posts on Instagram and Facebook. Carney's father, Mick, had been killed by a distracted driver. Her brother later found Mick's bucket list—sixty items in total, some of which he had ticked off before his untimely and tragic death. Carney in her grief decided to complete the list, which allowed her to craft a book in the process. A book that came to me and I was moved to review. My subsequent review was less about the work itself, and more about the feeling of loss.

I was once contacted by an editor at a national publication who said, "hey, you're the dead dad guy, right, I have an assignment that's perfect for you." He thought of me as the dead dad guy because I'd written about my father's death after having been pitched on crafting an essay collection about being a father. As I wrote the essays for what would become my book, *Lost in Space*, I intended to focus on my relationship with my young children. I found, however, that I couldn't escape my father's presence, much less his absence.

The piece I was assigned to write was about the author, television personality, and documentary filmmaker Yogi Roth, who was then promoting his new documentary *Life in a Walk*. The film is about Roth's efforts to spend time with his father, Will, as the latter faces a second bout of prostate cancer. Yogi's idea was to film he and his father taking a walk along the Carmen de Santiago in Portugal and Spain. Yogi hoped that his movie, as well as the piece I was writing, would prompt people to call their fathers while they were still alive. I can't call my father, much less make a movie with him. Laura Carney can't call her father, either. However, in working through her grief, something Yogi was doing as well—though spoiler alert, Will lived—Carney found her voice as an author. Writing essays about fatherhood didn't help me find my voice per se; it did, however, show me that dipping into nonfiction was a possibility.

All of which speaks about how we become artists and creatives. Immersion in grief is a medium for discovery and at times a path forward—I was trying to discover something about the past with *Lost in Space*, while also finding a way to get to whatever came next.

I interviewed Yogi for the piece, then for my podcast, and met him in Los Angeles while I was visiting the city. While he didn't work nine to five, he still worked every day. He wasn't creative all the time; he was, however, regimented with his time. I thought that maybe I needed to embrace this kind of life, where one consciously recognizes that working and creating can coexist—not one or the other, something I was already doing, though not formally, and not with a sense of calm acceptance. Still, I realized if I wasn't as successful as I wanted it to be, I still had my family, my health, goals, and direction.

It was then that I wondered if maybe I'd already figured something out and just thought I was looking for something else? That feeling trapped was more of an emotional thing than an actual physical manifestation of living that way. Maybe it was about staying the course, keeping it interesting, and embracing what I had and pushing myself to achieve to create more—to live more like Yogi Roth than Paul Hackett. That I'd be fired from my day job shortly thereafter and decide to reinvent myself as what I am now—hustler, teacher, coach, strategist, writer, trainer— means that I live more consciously like Yogi than I ever did when I was questioning how it all might work.

~

Back in February 1992, when I was reading *Don Juan* and just delving into journaling, I wrote something that must have seemed profound at the time to my twenty-four-year-old self:

> I've always felt that art could only find fruition if it was born of struggle. That one could only create if they were mired in angst and tension. Where else could a catalyst be found, but in the nether regions of the abyss? And yet I long to create, but don't suffer that much. Well at least not in a Kafkaesque sort of way. I don't feel psychological pain, I'm not haunted by terrors past. There is no hulking father or domineering mother. I haven't struggled with drugs or drink, if anything I've probably benefited from them. And yet, there is something I want to put down, a story I want to tell, a tale I want to share. Maybe I just want to create and feel I can't come up with something.

This passage was followed later that week by a loosely paraphrased quote from the movie *Naked Lunch*: "We all suffer, but writers report it."The actual quote, which is uttered by the character Exterminator #2 is "Just remember this. All agents defect, and all resistors sell out. That's the sad truth, Bill. And a writer? A writer lives the sad truth like anyone else. The only difference is he reports it."

I was close.

This was during a period when I wondered if I should go to law school. Another journal entry from that time referenced a quote from Kafka: "29 reasons not to go to law school... Lawyers: 'Persons who write a 10,000 word document and call it a brief.'"

That spring I moved to New York, and was having dreams where I was lost somewhere in the city, hanging out with people smoking weed and being herded into a building by a security guard who placed my finger in a machine that drained vital information from me and generated a report about what I do not know. I felt trapped, my hand was mangled, and I yelled out, "Am I in Kafka's *Trial* for god sakes?" I then grabbed the report and ran into the dark city streets. (I should mention that I had caught my hand in a lawnmower in the summer of 1987. At first my fingers were merely a traumatic and bloody mess—later I had to have a fingertip amputated.)

In late March of 1992, I wrote:

I seem to have left the Kafkaesque, *After Hours* paranoia trip through hell dream theme and entered some sort of displaced, woman from that past, but who I would have hooked-up with [vibe]…

Both Paul Hackett, and not.

The move to New York was one of *After Hours* displacement at first. It then shifted to untangling the reality of what it meant to return home—a place I'd chosen to leave behind, and now a place where I was forced to encounter the past and the unresolved vicissitudes of my earlier life.

Or some version of that.

~

Did Debbie and I watch movies during the two years we lived in New York—the bridge between my life in San Francisco where my desire to write began to take shape, and Chicago where it happened? Indeed, we did. Did we watch some Scorsese films? Indeed, we did.

Here are a few of them:

1. *The Age of Innocence*. Scorsese does old New York and Edith

Wharton. The stars were Daniel Day Lewis and Michelle Pfeifer, yet Winona Ryder stole the show, as she tended to do back then.

2. *Brother's Keeper.* A documentary about two brothers living on an isolated farm in upstate New York who may have killed a third brother and may have had a sexual relationship. Among the highlights is a Roscoe Diner bumper sticker on their tractor—a place I loved to visit as a child.

3. *Jurassic Park.* Debbie and I went to see this somewhere on the Upper West Side one weekday afternoon and emerged from the darkness of the theater into the glaring sun spellbound from a near pitch-perfect movie-going experience.

4. *Husbands and Wives.* An engrossing piece of manipulation as an artist crafts the version of a story they want the world to believe regardless of the actual truth. Mia Farrow is fantastic and tragic.

5. *Basic Instinct.* I watched this with Debbie the first weekend I returned to New York from San Francisco—we were technically on Long Island, but I was back. Sharon Stone may

have been nominated for an Oscar for Scorsese's *Casino* a few years later, but this is no question her greatest performance.

6. *Amongst Friends.* I don't believe this movie has had much staying power, nor was it well received when it came out. It's about a group of friends on Long Island who come from stable, striving homes and seek out a life of petty crime because it seems more exciting than going to college or living a straight and normal life. It's no *Mean Streets*, as my father might have said. And yet, it was one of the indie films coming out in the early 1990s, some of which were made by people Debbie and I might have gone to college with, and she might have grown-up with on Long Island. *The Brothers McMullen* is another such movie, though it came out just a little later and after we'd moved to Chicago. It was written and directed by Edward Burns, son of Queens, and a dude who lived on our quad freshman year of college.

7. *Bad Lieutenant.* Abel Ferrarra does Scorsese, religion and crime. It's sordid and grimy, and Harvey Keitel finally gets his *Apocalypse Now* moment. Scorsese considers it one of the best movies of the 1990s.

8. *Short Cuts.* A movie I found as engrossing as anything we watched during our New York years. It begat my reading *What We Talk About When We Talk About Love*, followed by everything else I could find by Raymond Carver, the author whose work impacted my early writing as much as anyone I was reading then, with nods to Andre Dubus, and as always, Jim Carroll.

If Naked Lunch was the movie that solidified for me how much I needed to write, *Short Cuts* is the film which confirmed it. That I didn't write a single sentence while we lived in New York City is only acceptable because I got started in Chicago—and after I got started, I never stopped.

~

I'll pause here to take another beat on *Amongst Friends*. As I mentioned, it's not great cinema, but it is reflective of what some people my age in the early 1990s were doing when we lived in New York City—including making movies, which I wanted to be around and part of, and wasn't. The thing is, Ed Burns really did live in the same dorm we did freshman year of college, before leaving school to make movies, or figure out how to anyway. And Rob Weiss, the writer and director of *Amongst Friends*, was a guy who knew guys Debbie grew-up with, including Doug Ellin, the creator of "Entourage," which Weiss worked on. Ellin based the character of director Billy Walsh on Weiss, even offering Weiss the role, which he declined. Then there's my friend Adam Lawrence, who worked on independent movies such as *Burnzy's Last Call*, which starred some of his classmates from SUNY Purchase— including Sherry Stringfield, who become a television star thanks to *ER*. A movie where Adam invited me to come visit him on the set, which I didn't because I decided I couldn't skip out on work.

Why are these things important? Because they were happening around me, and involved people I knew, or could have easily known, while I was still journaling about how and when I was going to get started.

In April 1992, I wrote about an insight I'd ruminate on for years—and still do:

> ...let's talk about my pop. I have fears, doubts, negative thoughts and questions about relationships lately. I never really did before...I certainly feel much of this angst is due to my perceptions of my father. I don't want to feel like he feels at times. At least in regard to family and obligation and failure. I don't question he

loves us, and needs us, but marriage and family have been a sort of negative influence on his work I believe. Kafka like you see. Now maybe it's been a convenient excuse for him. Fear of failure, of not being accepted or respected or liked, has been repressed, and he can say, well the wife, the kids, blah, blah, blah. I think he feels he would have done something differently, made some different choices. My fears and doubts may fully stem from this. I don't feel ready yet. Not stable enough. Haven't done all the things I want. I don't want to feel myself becoming secure until I want to be.

I go on to write about marriage, something Debbie and I weren't even considering at the time, and how "it shouldn't be like a prison." I've always sought security and stability, but I've never felt trapped during my marriage. Yet, a desire for security and stability can get in the way of living a creative life when it leads to an unwillingness to take chances and the question of whether you're all in—because if you're not, are you any different than Paul Hackett?

~

Movies, writing, creative life; I'm in it now. Yet am I in it enough? If not, what would that look like? This speaks to ambition, in general, and mine specifically. Is being a doer and a hustler the same thing as having ambition? I ask this as I sit in a Foxtrot, drinking coffee, reading *Story of a Poem* by Matthew Zapruder while waiting for Myles to finish an exam, which, if he passes, will allow him to become a student teacher. Myles has until December to take and pass the exam—it's June and he wants it done now. He wants the idea of it out of his head, which is less about ambition than anxiety. Yet Myles also knows that even when he questions his career path, he wants to teach when he's done with college, and that feels like ambition to me.

When I was his age, twenty-one, I had no idea what I wanted to do. Possibly something with television or movies, but no real clue about what, and no plan for how to figure that out.

My father knew what he wanted to do though.

Scorsese knew.

And Myles does too.

Last night Debbie, Myles and I went to see *Past Lives*, a beautiful looking and acted movie about two childhood friends in South Korea who are separated as children when the family of the female protagonist, Nora, emigrates to Canada. The move is related to ambition—South Korea is too small for Nora's parents' dreams and desires. But the question that arises is whether it's also too small for her? Nora and Hae Sung— the male protagonist—will reconnect twelve years later online and then twelve years after that in person in New York, where Nora is a playwright married to a writer.

At its most basic, *Past Lives* is about love, though more deeply, about destiny and timing, but also connections across time and space, and more mundanely, though still critical, the choices we make and those we don't. Nora's parents are artists—her father is a filmmaker—and they wanted more, as did Nora. When her classmates in South Korea ask why she's moving, Nora says it's because South Koreans don't win the Nobel Prize for Literature. When Nora and Hae Sung first reconnect, he asks her what prize she wants to win now? The Pulitzer, she replies. Later, when Hae Sung visits her in New York City, their prior online connection having been abandoned when Nora says she needs to focus on writing, not looking at flights to Seoul, he asks the question again. Nora says she doesn't think about those things anymore, before laughing and answering, that she wants to win a Tony. That night in a bar, with Nora's husband, Arthur, sitting next to him, Hae Sung says to Nora that she had to leave South Korea because it wasn't big enough for her ambition. Was that truly the case, despite what she said as a child, and does it matter regardless? Their connection and their love have been transformed and twisted in endless ways by timing, destiny, and choice, and her ambition to create is a force in her life as powerful as any feelings of love. Even that which she feels for Hae Sung or Arthur. Is that level of ambition required to achieve what one wants, and can it happen in any other way?

At one point, as Nora and Arthur lay in bed, he asks if this is how she imagined it—meeting some Jewish guy at a residency, having sex because you're both there, moving in together because you both live in New York, getting married because you need a green card, and ending up in some shitty apartment in the East Village? She replies, what about love? You left out that I love you. I know you do, he says.

I'm struck by Nora's ambition, and yes, the love in a shitty apartment which allows that ambition to be what it'll be.

Could I have done that?

I lived in a shitty apartment in New York. I chose to make less money than I might have—and much less than I made in San Francisco—to do what I wanted to do, which was working as a caseworker at a nonprofit. This was intentional.

I was making plans, willing to sacrifice, wanting to learn, feel something, be inspired, and in service.

Was that my ambition then?

Yes.

Did I also want to create an artistic life?

Yes.

Was I doing so?

No.

Myles sent me a one sentence review of *Past Lives* from Letterboxd, a platform where people share their reviews and feelings about movies: "The kinda movie that makes you want to sit down and write a book about your life."

Isn't that what I'm doing here? Using *After Hours* as a springboard to say something about art and living a creative life?

Yes.

I'm trying to, anyway.

Is it a coincidence that I interviewed Laura Carney about *My Father's List* and she told me how she wanted to write a book for years—as did her father—and how her first book is about her father's death and her ambition to achieve his thwarted ambitions?

Story of a Poem is a version of this story as well, as Zapruder writes about the act of composing a poem in all its tortured beauty. It's also the story of a writer seeking to understand his relationship with art and the world, and as a father looking to connect with his son who is neurodivergent. A story about life and what we make of it. A life that looks like Nora's and mine in how that life is about words and what they mean to us. From *Story of a Poem*:

> I have always loved words for what they can do, and for all the different things they can mean. I love how they feel in my mouth. In that way, I am like all writers I know. I am also very much like my son. Now that I have become the parent of a son who is working so hard to achieve fluency in language, my respect for communication in all aspects of my life has increased.

We, artists, humans, all of us, are trying to communicate about something.

For Scorsese it's about family, honor, and connection.

For Nora it's about the journey across time and place.

For Carney it's about love, grief, and voice.

For Zapruder it's about story, creativity, and grace.

~

In April 1992, I stumbled onto a quote by Akira Kurosawa that I wrote about in my journal: "A man is a genius when he's dreaming." One of Kurosawa's final movies was *Dreams*, which came out in 1990. It was a movie my father encouraged me to watch. *Dreams* comprises a series of eight vignettes, shot through with magical realism and a tangle of narratives which explore spirituality, art, and death. One vignette portrays an art student who loses himself in the work of Van Gogh—the actual work. Van Gogh is portrayed by none other than Martin Scorsese.

While Roger Ebert didn't review *Dreams*, he did write that "Kurosawa's late films were the meditations of an old man at peace." While it's hard to imagine Scorsese at peace, it's not hard to find Ebert's thoughts on *After Hours*, which he wrote about in his book, *Scorsese By Ebert*:[22]

> *After Hours* approaches the notion of pure filmmaking; it's a nearly flawless example of—itself. It lacks, as nearly as I can determine, a lesson or message, and is content to show the hero facing a series of interlocking challenges to his safety and sanity.

Ebert goes on to write that:

[c]ritics have called it "Kafkaesque" almost as a reflex, but that is a descriptive term, not an explanatory one…The film has been described as dream logic, but it might as well be called screwball logic; apart from the nightmarish and bizarre nature of his experiences, what happens to Paul Hackett is like what happens to Buster Keaton: just one damned thing after another.

Ebert also remarks how "the film could be read as an emotional autobiography of that period in Scorsese's life," which we already know, and how in the original version, Paul Hackett dies at the end of the movie, which I didn't know, though as Ebert shares, "Scorsese said he showed that version to his father, who was angry: 'You can't let him die!'" Ebert also writes that Scorsese called *After Hours* "an exercise completely in style." Ebert didn't agree and wrote in response: "But he could not quite hold it to that. He had to make a great film because, perhaps, at that time in his life, with the collapse of *The Last Temptation*, he was ready to, he needed to, and he could."

There's so much going on here, not the least of which is how I'm writing this on Father's Day, a day which I can celebrate and yet not help but ruminate on death—my father's, Paul Hackett's, almost, and my own.

My journal entries from the 1990s speak to my own emotional biography. How all of it's so limited. The "it" being the time we have on earth to live and create. The entries also speak about my desire to do something great. In the journal entry about Kurosawa, I also write about *The Trial* by Kafka, as it had been mentioned in an article I read at the time about poethics—law and ethics as encountered in literature. The article was about how Kafka found peace through writing and how writing allowed him to escape. I proceed to beat myself up on the pages of my journal for not better understanding these ideas and incorporating them into the thesis I wrote on Kafka my senior year in college. I didn't show myself much grace then, though I concluded the entry by writing, "What was I thinking that fall? Where was my vision? Life is a work in progress, and I guess my vision on this topic will grow as my awareness does."

~

In *Story of a Poem*, Zapruder writes about how when

attending graduate school for poetry, he found "fellow poets…who deeply mattered" to him and that "it would be a long time before I really understood [that] these connections mattered in life and in writing." He continues, "I began to think about them while I was writing…on the one hand, I felt a growing freedom and understanding of the composition process, which could sometimes be dizzying. On the other, there was the actual physical presence of readers who gave direction to that freedom."

Connection.

Freedom.

Dizziness.

Story.

Does Scorsese feel these things when he makes movies and works with his old friends and colleagues?

De Niro.

Pesce.

Now DiCaprio.

Is it dizzying for him to make a movie like *Goodfellas*, which never stops moving—the violence, humor, and story propulsive, constant, and sprayed across the screen—or *After Hours*, where all those same actions apply, even if the film is about dislocation, disorientation, and the desire to break free from that which traps us?

I thought about this on Father's Day as I insisted my family watch *The Cape*. It's the latest documentary by Yogi Roth and reflects so much about what this week is and has been. Reading *My Father's List* begot a review where I namedropped Yogi and *Life in a Walk*, which begot a text to Yogi to let him know about said reference, which was also a desire to connect with Yogi, who I rarely talk to—not that we ever spoke a lot. The text begot a lengthy back and forth with Yogi about writing and children and life—Yogi's now a father, and his father is still alive. The exchange concluded with an invitation to the premiere of *The Cape*, should I be in Los Angeles, which I wasn't, though with the film also dropping on Amazon Prime, Debbie, the boys, and I can watch it.

The movie was eight years in the making, which nearly spans the length of my friendship with Yogi, *Life in a Walk* having been released just over seven years ago. *The Cape* is Yogi's effort to trace a journey his great-great-great grandfather took by boat around Cape Horn in 1857, a journey captured in a journal passed from his great-great-great grandfather down the family line until it reached an eight-year-old Yogi, who became captivated by the story—journals as inspiration and connection, for Yogi, his great-great-great grandfather, me, and Jim Carroll. Yogi decided to re-trace his great-great-great grandfather's path with four strangers—a filmmaker, the two co-captains of the ship he hires, and a young Frenchman who happened to be in the area and joined them at the last minute. In creating the film, Yogi has both fulfilled a dream and added a chapter to a story that has been passed down through the generations.

For Yogi, the realization on this journey is that life is full of moments—one after the other, and each of which must be maximized. And that the greatest adventures are never done alone, that we all come from somewhere, that we all have a story, and it's okay to seek out these things. Adventure and story happen when we escape the house, or at least our heads.

Writing this book has been an adventure for me. A series of moments, a story about telling the story about how we create, find our voice, and freedom, however we define it.

Yogi went back to his great-great-great grandfather's journal and Cape Horn.

I went back to *After Hours*.

One journey is much cooler than the other, yet we find ourselves in the same place: storytellers seeking to share the stories of the people we feel connected to, which further compels us to be seekers who endlessly want to discover our voice, while never wanting to feel trapped—certainly not by ourselves. It's also about telling the story of our own lives, no matter how long it takes and no matter how far we must go to find it.

INTERVIEW with Yogi Roth

Ben Tanzer: To start, do you mind introducing yourself and telling us—and this is a big question in your case—who you are and what you do.

Yogi Roth: Of course. My name is Yogi Roth. And I think my position in the world is to seek and uncover the humanity within it, specifically through sports. And that's the lens in which I see all of life, from college football to documentaries, to writing to fatherhood, to friendship, to being a husband. And I'm a psycho competitor. I love sports and I love everything that sports can embody and release from somebody that maybe they don't know. That's what makes live sports so fun for me as a broadcaster and a filmmaker.

BT: I really love how you introduced yourself, because it's exactly how I think of you. But what's interesting is I met you because of the dad thing you shot, which was *Life in a Walk*, yet you only talked a little bit about making movies in your introduction. I'm curious, for you, what is it about making movies?

YR: For me, it all started in 2009 when I made my first film, *Three for the Show*, which was an ESPN documentary on quarterbacks. I'd had a coach call me and say, "Hey, our quarterback decided not to enter the NFL draft." You should do a movie on him. I had just left coaching after coaching quarterbacks for four years. I had done content at USC under Coach Pete Carroll, but I had never made anything other than a short that we played to the team before training camp that was meant to be inspiring. But nothing with gravitas. I called my contacts at ESPN and said that I thought I had something that could be a movie. They said, wow, this sounds cool, and what I learned was that access is such a big part of making movies. We hired an incredible director named John Hawk, and I said, all right, John, I want you to teach me how to turn the camera on. I already knew how to deal with athletes in locker rooms and what to shoot, when to shoot, when to ask questions, when to mic up a shoulder pad, whatever. But I didn't know anything about the craft and that was my first experience as a filmmaker. From that point on, I was hooked.

What I think I learned the most was, that for me, as a storyteller, we always have a part of our world in everything we touch, how we see the world, how we experience the world. *Life in a Walk*, of course, is very intimate. I needed to not have any regrets about my dad's life and to understand why he was living, what he hoped he would leave if God forbid he was dying, and how I was not okay with the idea of learning about him from somebody else. I made *The Cape* because I was obsessed with Cape Horn, which was the most dangerous place in the world for a sailor, which my great-great-great grandfather sailed in 1857 and 1858. I knew I was an explorer. I had to tap into my roots and my DNA. I wanted my life to make more sense…I think the more vulnerable the film, the more the audience can watch it and reflect vulnerably onto their own life versus getting to know yours.

BT: It's funny because the one very conscious thing I did with this book and choosing *After Hours* was to see if it would help me understand my dad better, or at least understand my grief as related to my dad. You talk about fathers, you mentioned your wife to me before we were recording, you mentioned your sons. You have a beautiful family, but you lead a creative life. I must admit, you're the first person I met where I thought, oh, there's a way to do that. I'm not sure Yogi's got a formula I can copy, but he's an actual human who's doing it. Do you think of your life as a creative one and how do you go about ensuring you get to live like you want to live?

YR: I believe all my creative endeavors have led me to the next one, but most importantly led me to the greatest thing in my life, which is *Life in a Walk*. If you recall, there's a scene in the movie where we kind of flipped the script and my dad asked me one question, which is, are you going to spend time with somebody? And I got embarrassed, and said, I'm really looking for three things, I want somebody who's smart, I want somebody who can bust my chops and is intelligent, and I want somebody with a great smile. I met my wife on a plane. I sat next to her and met all three of those things. She went home and within a couple of weeks watched *Life in a Walk* and she said, yes, she knew it. That it was us. So, every creative endeavor has led me to the next one, but also led me to my wife, which led me to our sons, which led me to my family.

There was a point that really hit me that my goal and my

objective is to live a full life. I want a myriad of experiences, and that's what I'm going to compete to do. And the things that light up my soul the most are seeking and uncovering, especially around story. My greatest trait is the one that I go to when I need it the most, which is writing. Everything else takes a lot of work and a lot of practice and a lot of preparation. But writing, I can just go…I started writing when I was ten years old. I didn't want to tell anybody else my dreams, so I started to journal. I've never stopped, and journaling became the avenue to a film or an avenue to a new book or an avenue to start up a podcast or an avenue to a pitch. That's just how I want to live. As I've gotten older, I found out what matters most to me and I believe the greatest performers, the greatest competitors, the greatest organizations, understand what matters most with great clarity, with confidence and discipline. What matters most to me is performing, ideating, creating. I know I can do those things, and then you must have a disciplined approach to attacking it.

~

Spending as much time as I have thinking about inspiration, generations, cinema, and fathers, I asked Myles what his favorite movies are. He sent me the following via Google docs:

TOP TEN MOVIES OF ALL TIME

About Time is the perfect romance movie because even though there is a scientific element to it, it shows realistic love between two amazing performances. The father-son dynamic is just heart wrenching. And you also have Margot Robbie in her third movie role ever.

Booksmart is easily the best high school movie of the last ten years. It's just a smart, well-written script and I love that the cast is actors who are up and coming. *Booksmart* just makes you smile. Also, Billie Lourd was robbed of an Oscar nomination.

Drop Dead Gorgeous is easily the funniest movie ever. It brings my two favorite genres together, mockumentary and high school. The ensemble is AMAZING; Kirsten Dunst, Denise Richards, Amy Adams, Brittany Murphy, Allison Janney, Kirstie Alley, and Ellen Barkin.

Hairspray truly changed my life and deepened my

love for Zac Efron. I just love movies that at the end of the day make you feel something, and *Hairspray* truly does. Also, you have Amanda Bynes singing, so what could be better?

Inside Out is an exceptional movie for children because it makes them think about their mental health in a way they can understand and comprehend, but at the same time it's just wholesome. Who knew you could care so much for some eight-year-old girl's emotions and old imaginary friend that you just sob.

Interstellar
Never in a million years had I thought a true science fiction movie would be on my top ten movie list, but *Interstellar* changed that. I don't even know what they are saying most of the time, but you want them to save the world, and you want everything to be happy and it's done by some of the best performances ever.

Mean Girls is my favorite movie of all time, and I don't think there will ever be any competition. I have easily watched it over fifty times, and I can recite most of the dialogue. I enjoy that it tries to be realistic, but not a parody either. Even though *Mean Girls* came out in 2004, it is still relevant now.

Parasite is my second favorite movie of all time, but I tell "movie people" it's my favorite. It perfectly shows how the working class and first class interact and how they affect each other in ways that are so impressive. I fell in love with it when I first watched the movie and realized the trailer gives you absolutely nothing at all.

Pitch Perfect is a movie that is pure smiles and happiness given through the gift of girl power, singing, and comedy. There is truly no bad part or character in the movie. It's just a laugh out loud, good feel movie. The ending of *Pitch Perfect* will go down as one of the greatest scenes and musical moments of all time.

Someone Great is the most realistic millennial romance movie ever. It shows three women who are going through their own romance shit but still help each other out. You just root for them and cry for them. It also reminds me of my favorite show, *Broad City*, so it can't be bad.

While Myles' list includes only a smattering of the movies we've seen together, and excludes many we love—where's *Up* or *Jackie*—the only omission I want to note is *Hugo* by Scorsese. It came out in 2011 when Myles was nine. I took him to see it because I wanted to watch it in a theater and could best justify disappearing on a Saturday afternoon to go to a movie back then if I took a child with me. I also wanted to introduce Myles to Scorsese, and because *Hugo* is Scorsese's ode to the magic of the movies and their impact on his life, while I hoped Myles would love Scorsese, what I really wanted was for him to love movies—to see how one can lose themselves in their storytelling and power, knowing there's a place where one can go to escape and find awe. Myles didn't love *Hugo* and as it turns out, it's Noah who loves Scorsese movies, especially *The Wolf of Wall Street*. However, Myles does love movies, embracing them as a means for living and thinking about life, which is all I wanted anyway.

~

In April 1992, I journaled the following:

Do you make yourself write every day? Like you would like to make yourself run every day? So, it would feel smoother, so that the ideas would flow with veritable ease, so you could lock into your rhythm that much faster? Does writing even work like that? Does it feel more fluid and brilliant as the days pass? Does the mind and body work in similar ways? If so, do you need to stretch mentally as you do physically? And contra positively do you atrophy, feel tighter, and less flexible, if you take time off? What sort of approach should I even take? I act like I will get myself to run every day, and yet I don't, though it is something I enjoy. When I don't, I say, well I don't want to make myself do this, it really is for pleasure. Will I, do I, take the same approach to writing? Should I push myself at both? See how far I can go?

Then five months to the day I wrote my first journal entry (January 11, 1992), in which included my friend Pete's comment, "At least you're killing time in a pseudo-productive way," I wrote the last entry in that journal and referenced that comment.

I still didn't believe I agreed with Pete's sentiment.

Yet, it lingered.

Now living in New York City, I was taking a philosophy class, and when the topic of drug use arose, something I acknowledged freely engaging in while hitting a certain peak usage in San Francisco I'd never repeat, the teacher asked, "It was a free ride, wasn't it?" in reference to the insights, visions, and bliss I'd experienced.

I'm not sure I agreed with that either. I didn't feel I'd tapped into anything that was achieved via shortcut.

Yet, it lingered.

I was in motion at that point, churning and yearning to be something and someone else—a creative being. I also quoted from Kafka in that final May journal entry:

You don't need to leave your room. Remaining sitting at your table and listen. Don't even listen, simply wait. Don't even wait. Be quite still and solitary. The world will freely offer itself to you. To be unmasked, it has no choice. It will roll in ecstasy at your feet.

I really wanted to believe this, as it's in essence the opposite of what drives Paul Hackett.

In *After Hours* to leave your room is a necessity.

It's everything.

It's how one finds one's life force.

I was much more Paul Hackett then.

Driven to be outside, to see what was possible.

I journaled about my life, and I explored my fears and desires, as I sought to forge some kind of creative path. But I didn't do then what I do every day now, thirty years hence, and literally at this moment as I sit here in a hotel room in Big Sky, Montana, my last day of a work trip, a world of possibility outside my window. I'm up early, the sun rising, so I can write.

I'm still searching.

I'm also a writer.

Period.

~

I remain in transition from my time in the mountains, where I worked, slept, hiked, wrote, and ran, things I try to do every day, especially when I'm traveling for work. I reflect on that last day in Montana, and how I shifted from my early morning writing about journals, Kafka, and Paul Hackett to running in the mountains of Big Sky.

As I ran, I listened to the Otherppl with Brad Listi podcast, where Brad is interviewing Bea Sutton, a fellow runner and obsessive. As they spoke about the protagonist in Sutton's debut novel, *Berlin*, Sutton and Listi discussed how the character doesn't take advantage of the club scene in Berlin. This led to an exchange about the romanticization of writing, late nights, and drinking, and how such a lifestyle is not truly amenable to getting the work done. Listi then referenced a quote by Flaubert I've returned to again and again during the writing of this book, "Be regular and orderly in your life, so that you may be violent and original in your work."

The sentiment behind this quote has stuck with me since I first heard it at the beginning of my writing career. My interpretation of it has been to be as boring as possible to ensure I get the work done. My approach to writing is that it must be viewed through the lens of any job I have—focused, scheduled, not precious or serving at the whim of inspiration, though inspiration should be followed when it presents itself.

Once, when Myles was mad at me, he said, "...and you're so fucking boring, too," and I thought good, that's the goal. I want to create and do cool stuff while ensuring we have health insurance, retirement and college funds, and that the bills are paid. Being boring is key to accomplishing all this.

I once drank a lot. I also took a lot of drugs. From the ages of fourteen to thirty it was a regular way of life for me.

At the time, it was hard to understand if it was problematic—though of course it was. I just didn't know how much. I thrived academically in college. I was an athlete. Later, I always got up for my job and excelled once there. I continued to compete as an athlete. I had mostly healthy relationships. My worst impulses weren't pursued, most of the time. Things that were important to me didn't go away. I had fun. A lot of it. Addiction and alcoholism don't run in my family. Still, I also got lucky. I frequently blacked out, which was a problem, though that wasn't always clear to me why when I could go to work, excel, exercise, and on and on.

Then I wanted to stop.

Some of that was age.

Some of that was the result of shame—I blacked out in front of a new friend who seemed horrified as he asked if this was a regular thing for me. Most of my friends before then had treated it as normal. It was normal for them. It was our normal.

It wasn't only shame, however. I had a therapist say to me, "it doesn't work for you anymore." What he meant, and what it meant to me, was that this lifestyle worked if I was focused on school, jobs, sex, sports, reading, and watching movies—and it didn't work if I was going to pursue bigger dreams and create. I needed my evenings, my early mornings, my weekend afternoons, and the excessive use of drugs and alcohol and their unpredictable outcomes no longer served me. Being regular and orderly did, especially as I moved from journaling to sitting down, pen in hand, and tried to craft something, anything, that looked like writing, which I've now done for three decades.

~

One more thought on Flaubert.

In 2017, Nick Ripatrazone wrote an article for LitHub titled, "30 Years Later, Scorsese Makes His *Silence.*"[23] Ripatrazone writes about how Scorsese purchased the film rights for the book, *Silence,* which was published in 1966, after the Reverend Paul Moore, the Episcopal Bishop of New York, gave Scorsese a copy in 1988. This was after the release of *The Last Temptation of Christ* and the criticism Scorsese received for the film in "Christian circles." It would take Scorsese thirty years to make *Silence.* Ripatrazone compares this to Flaubert's writing of *The Temptation of Saint Anthony,* which he finished in 1872, but had started thirty years before.

In the article, Ripatrazone also mentions that Michel Foucault wrote that the idea for *The Temptation of Saint Anthony* "was repeated—as ritual, purification, exercise, a 'temptation' to overcome—prior to writing each of his major texts." Ripatrazone adds that Flaubert was "nearly ecstatic writing it," and quotes Flaubert himself: "I spend my afternoons with the shutters closed, the curtains drawn, and without a shirt, dressed as a carpenter. I bawl out! I sweat! It's superb…I have never been more excited."

Sounds like Kafka.

Maybe Jim Carroll.

Certainly Scorsese.

Ripatrazone goes on to write that "*Silence* is a lamentation. More than 50 years later, it's finally a film in America—a film by the son of Sicilians, known for their own particular silence when it comes to God. A silence born by the skepticism of everyday struggles."

The struggle to believe in ourselves.

To find one's voice.

To create the work of one's entire life.

Sometimes we know what that work can or might be.

Most of the time we keep pushing, following a path the allows us to create, develop a approach that works for us— being regular and orderly, or not—as we hope for the best.

~

As I get on a plane to fly back home from Montana, I pick up *The Story of a Poem* again. I am quickly immersed in it, again. Though the book is ostensibly about writing a poem, it's also about Zapruder facing and embracing the life he has with his neurodivergent son. It's not the life Zapruder expected, and he writes how holding onto the life one imagined can ruin a person. The book is also the story of losing a parent, in this case Zapruder's father, and what it looks like to process that grief.

In one passage, Zapruder is in an airport, moving between planes and those liminal spaces we enter as we do, when a phrase comes to him: "Come on, all you ghosts." Zapruder knew this moment would lead to the creation of a poem, which he started writing in his head as he got off the plane and into his car. Then he wrote the actual poem, or as he says, transcribed it, something Kafka and Flaubert would understand, as would countless artists over countless centuries—my father and Scorsese included. Zapruder then writes

> The phrase that bubbles up from my psyche was an incantation, a personal prayer. There was something about the rhythm of it that exactly embodied the form

I needed for my thoughts, and what I was so intensely feeling. Its rhythm made a shape which fit not only the poetry I needed to write, but how I needed to live now that my father was truly gone…'After great pain, a formal feeling comes,' Emily Dickinson wrote. She is referring to that initial stage of grief, but for poets this can mean the compulsion to find the exact form is language that captures the pain, not through the meaning of the words, but through the rhythm and sound and shape. As I wrote about my father, I felt my loss again become nearly real. I moved through it, now with some distance, which paradoxically brought pain that was just as intense, but also a genuine perspective that I could not have had in the first years after my father's death. I also thought of the people I had passed in New York and Houston and San Francisco and all the cities and towns we had driven through. Them, and also my friends, many of whom were gone from my life or life altogether. I know I was talking to them, and hopefully by extension to you. Writing a poem reminded me my continuing sorrow was not only not unique, but the most common thing in the world.

This book is about a movie I love by a director I love that allows me to explore my grief for someone I love in an ongoing fashion through the lens he loved most—art, the movies, and Scorsese, which as Zapruder says, hopefully speaks to you as well.

~

On September 30, 1998, I wrote the following as part of a much longer journal entry:

I have taken a new job…and I am pushing off into new directions…I wanted change and adventure when I hit 30. I wanted to experience new things and embrace risk and wonder…I also wondered how this move or any of the moves I've been trying to make fit contextually with where I've been and where I thought I would or should go. So, I revisited the old journals and the last several years of musings. I found a person, my younger self, living in California and contemplating how one opened doors and whether he was cruising through life. That person moved to New York City and the questions truly emerged. It was truly an introspective time in those early days; the [journal] writing is fast, and furious, and frequent. From San Francisco to New York City that person wrote all the time, searching, and quoting all those he encountered in print and person…He slept little and wrote much about it. He was obsessed with his dreams, and he struggled the most with this desire to write. The urge to put words on the printed page, and not just in journal form, but in the form of stories. Stories to be read and maybe published. He could never get himself to do it though and he constantly asked why…And now I write, I really do. I'm saddened that the younger guy couldn't find his way because it's a wonderful feeling, even the rejection letters. I think he would have had much to say, of course you have to be ready and so I don't dwell on it too much. I'm doing it now, and I'm writing many of the stories I thought about then.

When I started to write daily at the age of thirty, I started journaling less and less—and after this entry I never again journaled about my desire to write or create. I wrote about other things; my father's death, which became source material for my novel, *My Father's House*; a trip to Italy I took to grieve, and have an adventure before Debbie and I had children, which became a published essay; my own cancer misdiagnosis and the convoluted path for answers that followed, which became another essay; being caught far from home on September 11th and the subsequent twenty-six hour bus trip I took to get home, which I journaled about in real time, and also turned into an essay; and Myles birth, much of which, the impressions anyway, would become the basis for *Lost in Space*. The journaling fully petered out in August of 2002, ten years after I had started and five years before my debut novel, *Lucky Man*, would be published in 2007.

Until the pandemic, when I started again. At first, I was assigning journal prompts to my students as I regaled them about the benefits of journaling, how it brings focus, and enhances one's ability to be present. I soon wondered if I could benefit from doing so myself, again.

~

Wendy C. Ortiz's work entered my consciousness when she suddenly seemed omnipresent with her twisty and beautiful memoir, *Excavation*, which is about a relationship she had with a teacher fifteen years older than her, and someone placed alongside *Lost in Space* on a year-end top ten list. I soon found myself in the Strand Bookstore in New York, and there was *Excavation* awaiting my purchase. I bought the book with the intent of reading it at some point during a family trip I was on. Later that afternoon my body chilled, I began to hallucinate on the train ride to my in-law's home, and when I got there, I immediately climbed into bed, awaking the next morning in a fever dream—with *Excavation* on the floor next to the bed. I read it then and there, start to finish, in the throes of my illness, feverish, near crazed, and I can't imagine how anyone could experience the book and its exploration of teen darkness, and adult neglect and exploitation—the layers and insights endless, dreamy, fierce, and luminous—in any other way. It wouldn't release me from its feral grip, not once I got healthy again, or since. One thing I was gripped by was how Wendy had drawn on her teenage journals to tell the story. I'd done something similar with *My Father's House*, though that was fiction. *Excavation* was an eruption of personal narrative in its messy and triumphant glory. It was also nonfiction. A life lived and captured in real time.

Ortiz followed *Excavation* with *Hollywood Notebook*, which chronicles her time in Los Angeles and her efforts to become a writer—once again tracking her ongoing examination of self, desires, and dreams, once again drawing on her journals and notebooks to craft the story. If *Excavation* killed me, even as it spoke to things I hadn't experienced or understood, *Hollywood Notebook* spoke to something I well understood and wanted to capture myself, the birth of the artist. From the *Los Angeles Review of Books*, August 7, 2015:

> I'm a writer like so many other unknown writers all over this city. I have ordinary concerns, like paying rent on an apartment in Hollywood, the merry-go-round of moving my car twice a week for street cleaning, riding the Metro five days out of seven to a job, wondering about love and obsessing about sex and publishing and what will happen next.[24]

Shades of Jim Carroll, Patti Smith, Kafka, and Paul Hackett.

"What will happen next?"

Indeed.

INTERVIEW with Wendy C. Ortiz

Ben Tanzer: Would you mind briefly introducing yourself?

Wendy C. Ortiz: I'm a psychotherapist and the author of three books.

BT: I was particularly interested in talking to you because of the enormous impact your books have had on me. As I was trying to get the rhythm for this book on *After Hours*, I wouldn't say I was channeling *Excavation*—there's no way I could channel *Excavation*—except to say that you're someone who writes from your journals, and I wanted this book to feel like I was writing from a journal. So, I'm curious how you thought about that as you were writing *Excavation*, and how you think about your journals.

WCO: I feel like you're catching me at a very interesting time in terms of how I'm thinking about journals because I have recently been contemplating destroying many of my old journals.

BT: Whoa.

WCO: Yeah. And that's something that I never used to

imagine doing. I know plenty of people who do that, and on some level, I used to get it on an acceptance level. Like, okay, that's what you feel like you need to do. But I couldn't imagine doing it myself. However, in the last few years, I've started contemplating what that process would look like because I'm carrying around one massive trunk and three shelves of journals from age six to now, and besides the fact that it takes up a lot of room, what I'm finding is that when I go back to look at some of these journals, there's a lot of writing in there that I'm like, you know what, this actually doesn't need to be in existence anymore. I guess I'm also thinking too of my own mortality and the fact that my kid would inherit this stuff. Do I need my kid to be reading some of this stuff?

BT: I'm glad I'm catching you right now because I associate you with journals. It's you, Jim Carroll, Mike DeCapite. What's interesting is that when you talked about carrying it, I thought there's the physical carrying and there's also the emotional carrying, and I wondered, is that part of it too?

WCO: Absolutely, that's a big part of it. It's interesting to look at my journals from when I was twelve, because my kid is twelve. When I opened a journal yesterday to look at it from when I was that age, it still feels visceral, the things that were important to me. I may be coming from a bit of a place of judgment right now, but it would be sentimental to keep it at this point and I don't know if that's a good enough reason. There are also parts of my life where I'm like, I kind of lost my mind after my father died, and there are journal entries that I feel are for me only, and they can live in my body and in my memory, but nobody else needs to see them. And so, there is something about carrying them physically, but also some of these things I'm prepared to let go of emotionally.

BT: I know you've got a whole history of writing and art, but particularly with *Excavation*, did you think, I'm not going to be able to write this without my journal? Clearly, it's a memoir, but I know the journals played a big role in it for you.

WCO: I think it really goes back to my teacher telling me that I could not write about our relationship, though I was already journaling about it. So, I was already writing about the thing that I wasn't supposed to be writing about, according to him. I think that the young me at the time was already envisioning how it would be written as fiction, because I knew that it was a compelling story. I was living it, and I was like, this is something I'm not supposed to write about and I'm going to have to disguise all the details. But this is a really exciting story because I'm thirteen years old and this is the wildest thing that's ever happened to me. It was maybe not even a hundred percent conscious, but it definitely was at play as I continued journaling. Like this was all going to end up somewhere in some kind of writing. At the time, I always imagined it as fiction because it was too overwhelming to imagine writing a memoir. Also, back when I was fifteen, sixteen, memoir wasn't something that everybody was doing; if you were an artist, you were writing fiction. Later, when I was actively writing *Excavation*, I would go back to these journals. That's what they existed for at the time—to be able to go back and read about everything that I was feeling and the dates and what was happening.

BT: Even at thirteen you had this idea that you were going to write about the relationship with your teacher someday. Did you know at that age that you wanted to be an author or just that you had some great material?

WCO: I knew that I wanted to be a writer. I didn't know what that meant or what it looked like, but I knew that I was already writing. And it's funny because I wrote two novels when I was like fourteen, fifteen, and I found one of them yesterday that I'd completely forgotten about. The title is *Mischief* and it's just a composition book filled with some story I don't even remember writing. I'm a little scared to read it, but that's what I was doing. My parents were like, this is a great hobby, but I didn't have any idea of what it meant to be a writer. I'll get a regular job and then I'll write on the side whenever I have time, which is kind of how it ended up being. But I still conceived of myself as a writer. I just didn't know what that looked like in reality.

BT: That's the perfect segue to where I was going and offers an interesting stepping-stone to my final question. There's *Hollywood Notebook*, which I love. I just thought you would've been so fun to meet back then. You would've been in your twenties, right?

WCO: Yeah, late twenties.

BT: When you were moving from Olympia back to L.A., where you're from?

WCO: I had just moved back.

BT: And you're keeping journals, and the entries are very much about how you're going to become an artist. How does an artistic life even work? When I read a book like *Just Kids* or *Hollywood Notebook*, I'm think, how did these people do this? I say that with admiration, but what was that like, and in those journal entries, were you really trying to figure something out?

WCO: My therapist was always throwing this monkey wrench into the idea of a regular work life…You're a writer so why wouldn't you try to find part-time work and then have time to write? And I really resisted that for a long time because how can you do that? But then I was doing it, and I was able to do it much more easily in Olympia because of the cost of living there. Then when I moved to L.A. it was like, oh, I have to just swallow the reality that I have to work forty hours a week. I hadn't worked full-time in a while because I had always arranged these wonderful scenarios where I didn't have to work full-time, and I could still make ends meet. But in L.A. I had to work full-time. I got to a point where I was not writing and started to literally feel suicidal because I wasn't writing. And when I realized that my depression and my suicidal ideation was because I didn't have time to write, that was a massive wake up call. Like, oh my God, I need to figure out some other way to do this because I can't keep doing this the way I'm doing it. And that's kind of what *Hollywood Notebook* ended up being. Not the writing that I did when I took time off, but more like me flailing around suddenly unemployed, trying to figure out how to live and how to write and not doing it. I let life take over and suddenly my days were filled with weird errands and wasting time…Then I had to go back to work. I couldn't live that way forever. So, after three months, I got a part-time job, but from that point on I was like, I'm going to figure out a way to only work part-time so I have time to write. And I've done it ever since.

~

From my journal on December 31, 2022—mere days after I talked about the potential publication date for *After Hours: Scorsese, Grief and The Grammer of Cinema* with Ig, the publisher of this book:

And so, it is the last day of the year. The reflection,

assessment, and re-charge will come, maybe as soon as tomorrow, though more likely next week post-journey [we were driving to New Orleans in the new year]...I signed my 7.13 contract [for the novel *The Missing*] and locked in a fall 2024 date with Ig...I did not hear from Joanna [my agent] or Leah [a publisher I'm working with to re-issue *Lost in Space* and *Be Cool*]. I did awake to a note from Jerry on *Human Noise* [Jerry Brennan, the publisher of *Tortoise Books* and *Human Noise*, a new short story collection I've drafted], not great, but lots, lots to think about and while it wasn't unabashed love, and not that I should expect that, I found it exciting whether he's ultimately interested or not, which is also to say that I have work to do, it will take time, and good, I'm out of my head. There is work to do on *The Choice* [my next novel] as well. There will be work to do on *Midlife* [my next essay collection] too, no doubt. I thought I wanted all these to be done...and here we are, no closure, but movement and a near sense of peace. I'm in it, things are happening, that's what I wanted as much as anything. I need to slow down as well. I pushed and pushed, and will push more now, possibly tomorrow to finish this draft of *Completely Acceptable* [a novel I was inspired to write after watching *The Fabelmans*], then [the] trip, and slow. I would feel this way on some level anyway, but there is also the dream I had, my sleep wasn't without disruption. It's not totally coherent, it might have been an hour ago when I awoke, but what I know is that it was a day of being lost and confused in New York City. I was downtown, I was meeting Tara [someone I knew in college], why, I don't know, there was a museum, a car, which I was driving at some point in reverse, and felt I could not control [my persistent anxiety dream is one where whatever is else is going on I am in a car at some point and I lose control], then I misplaced it [the car], soon I was on an underground river hoping to go upstream and against the tide, on a couch that immediately sank, there was someone there, someone I was looking for and she was Millie Bobbie Brown [of *Stranger Things* fame], why, I don't know, and they disappeared, and I asked the station master if he had seen them, and he had not, and he was kind and stuff, and I dropped my phone in the water, and I lost all this time, and I couldn't figure out when or how, and that was most upsetting of all, where had it gone, had I blacked out, was it a mental health crisis, I did not know, and then I was home, with Debbie in some New York City apartment trying to explain it all, but I could not. And then I was awake, chilled and anxious…Now I'm here, slowing down, freaked, less freaked, and thinking, more sleep always means more anxiety dreams, yet here we are, and we've been pushing, and it's been all production and all anxiety, and it's time to slow down, for a minute, because all of that [the work and writing I was attempting to do by years-end] would need to be done, but maybe not quite like that, but still, done by week and year's end. So, yes here we are, mostly rested…work to do, lots, and so much promise too.

Literary things are happening and for so long it's what I wanted as much as anything. I'm talking about actual books with actual publishers and agents. I'm writing. Everyday. Journaling, too. I'm a creative being. I'm not trapped in an office like Paul Hackett. I'm not searching for something elusive— even if I still want so much and things still get overwhelming. Confusing. Day-to-day life can seem bleak and impossible to escape. I can feel anxious. And when I do, I still find myself dreaming about being lost somewhere in downtown New York City, trying to make sense of what's transpired, and seeking access and answers from those seemingly in a position of authority and unwilling to help. Like Paul Hackett, I'm still trying to escape my own head, and we always are.

~

I watched *After Hours* again, with Noah, because I wanted to end this book with one more viewing of the movie, ideally with a child of mine. I wanted the moment to be about the movies, this movie, *After Hours*, Scorsese, and the idea that I might share it with the next generation.

Also, one more list, the top ten movies I've watched while crafting this project:

1. *Women Talking*. A movie about violence that shows little violence—and a movie about the power of story and language.

2. *38 at the Garden*. The most New York City thing I may watch all year. It's a documentary about Jeremy Lin, the Knicks, Madison Square Garden, and Linsanity—beautiful, heartbreaking, and fleeting.

AFTER HOURS: AUTEUR

3. *Creed III.* Not as good as the first one, yet still visceral, celebratory, violent, and a movie I feel Scorsese would approve of. Regardless, the reviewers know that a homage to *Raging Bull* is required if one is going to talk about boxing movies. For example, this one from *Slug Magazine*:

> The original *Rocky* cemented the model for boxing movies and underdog sports movies in general. Martin Scorsese's *Raging Bull* in turn had an equally profound effect on the rest of the *Rocky* series with its visceral approach to sound editing and makeup effects upping the brutality in the ring. *Creed III*, the ninth film in the *Rocky* franchise, once again draws on Scorsese, this time from the 1991 thriller *Cape Fear*.[25]

Cape Fear. Interesting. And yet, it's right there—a person who feels wronged from one's past returns to terrorize them. The difference is how the story plays out. Jonathan Majors' Dame is far more sympathetic than De Niro's Max Cady— and this despite Majors' personal life encroaching on one's ability to feel any sympathy for him or a character he's playing.

4. *Air*. This is clearly a Ben Affleck movie with a terrific performance by Matt Damon, one of many terrific performances during Damon's now long career, including Scorsese's Oscar-winning *The Departed*.

5. *John Wick: Chapter Four*. Not so Scorsese at all—too cartoony, too much fantasy, though America's love for violence and crime coupled with Scorsese's love of honor—is none-the-less omnipresent.

6. *Rye Lane*. A delightful romantic comedy, funny, charming, and filled with breakout performances.

7. *Guardians of the Galaxy, Vol. 3*. With apologies to Scorsese and his clearly delineated feelings about Marvel movies, this was sad and moving, if not quite as good as the first in the series, which is still among the best of all Marvel movies.

8. *Past Lives*. You know how I feel about this one. Glorious and bewitching.

9. *The Cape*. I'm all Yogi Roth all the time, and happy to be so.

10. *After Hours.* I watched this twice as I worked on this project. First alone, late on a Friday night, post-tacos and a margarita, and now with Noah on a rainy Saturday afternoon. The film will always exhilarate and move me, as well as engender new observations, even as I know the beats and twists from start to finish.

This time, I noticed that Marcy describes her husband as a "movie freak," whose favorite film was *The Wizard of Oz*—which is one of Scorsese's favorites, which I only know because of the research I did for this book. Marcy's husband likes to yell "Surrender Dorothy!" every time he orgasms, which leads Marcy to leave him. Also, Paul constantly states how he just wants to get home. How hadn't I made the connection before?

Another observation: during the scene where the diner owner offers Paul and Marcy free coffee, he says, "Different rules apply when it's this late…it's after hours." A minor detail maybe, yet one I didn't recall until watching the film this time.

Meanwhile, Noah's reaction to the movie was thus:

"So this was *After Hours*? I was not expecting that. That was something. I like it…That's one of your favorite movies? That wiped me out."

Mission accomplished.

Two final thoughts.

At one point, Marcy says to Paul, "Well, here we are," and I thought, here we are at the end of this book.

And, at the end of the movie, Neil and Pepe find Paul wrapped in papier-mâché and mistake him for Kiki's sculpture from the beginning of the movie. We learn that Neil paid for the sculpture before Paul stole it from him and Neil wants it back.

Pepe says this is junk.

To which Neil responds that you don't understand that "art is forever."

I hope so.

ACKNOWLEDGMENTS

This starts and ends in its way with my great love for the work and many masterpieces of Martin Scorsese.

For New York City.

The Basketball Diaries.

Kafka.

Patti Smith.

These beginnings and endings only exist, however, because of my parents, Mike and Judy Tanzer, my brother Adam, my wife Debbie, our children Myles and Noah, lovers of story, cinema, and New York City all.

Adam Lawrence's presence in my life and on the page has been immeasurable (along with Eric Boime, paired as they've been in so many ways throughout my time on earth), as has been that of Yogi Roth, Wendy C. Ortiz, Mike DeCapite, Laura Carney, Gina Frangello, Brad Listi, Celine Song, Matthew Zapruder, and Jerry Stahl, too.

Which is to say I've been blessed to know, read, and absorb

many writers, filmmakers, and humans I love, who have in turn influenced me, this book, and the creative life I've been able to pursue.

So, this book is a product of all their light, and yet still wouldn't exist without Ryan W. Bradley who brought this project to my attention, and Robert Lasner who steered it to completion, what a gift they, and this book, have been for me.

NOTES

1. Matthew Jacobs, "Griffin Dunne Answers Every Question We Have About After Hours," *Vulture*, December 6, 2021, https://www.vulture.com/2021/12/after-hours-griffin-dunne.html.
2. Chris Nashawaty, "35 Years Ago, After Hours Saved Martin Scorsese's Career," *Esquire*, October 11, 2020, https://www.esquire.com/entertainment/movies/a34335663/after-hours-martin-scorsese-35th-anniversary-essay-history/
3. Koraljika Suton, "Martin Scorsese's Encounter with Kafka During After Hours," Cinephilia Beyond, June 18, 2022, https://cinephiliabeyond.org/after-hours/
4. Mike Fleming, Jr., "Martin Scorsese, Leonardo DiCaprio & Robert De Niro On How They Found The Emotional Handle For Their Cannes Epic 'Killers Of The Flower Moon,'" Deadline, October 20, 2023, https://deadline.com/2023/10/martin-scorsese-interview-killers-of-the-flower-moon-leonardo-dicaprio-robert-de-niro-1235359006/
5 J.M. Garrison, "Getting into the Cage: A Note on Kafka's "A Hunger Artist," *International Fiction Review*, 8, no. 1 (1981), https://journals.lib.unb.ca/index.php/IFR/article/view/13486
6. Nick De Semlyen, "The Irishman Week: Empire's

Martin Scorsese Interview," *Empire*, November 7, 2019,https://www.empireonline.com/movies/features/irishman-week-martin-scorsese-interview/

7. Pietro Mauri, "The 10 Best Movies Influenced By Franz Kafka," Taste of Cinema, November 13, 2025, https://www.tasteofcinema.com/2015/the-10-best-movies-influenced-by-franz-kafka

8. Albert Boime, "Michael Tanzer: An Artist Searching For His Routes," in *Michael Tanzer: A Life In Art, ed. Carol Gordon Wood*, (Roberson Museum and Science Center), 2001.

9. Sean Fennessey, "The Five Stages of Scorsese." The Ringer, December 23, 2016, https://www.theringer.com/2016/12/23/16047062/martin-scorsese-movies-50-years-72de1e5b173d

10. Roger Ebert, "I Call First / Who's That Knocking at My Door?," RogerEbert.com, November 17, 1967, https://www.rogerebert.com/reviews/i-call-first--whos-that-knocking-at-my-door-1967

11. Ibid.

12. Eileen Lavin, "Nobody Knows The Tsuris I've Seen." *Moment*, December 31, 2012, https://momentmag.com/jewish-word-tsuris/

13. Mike McGranaghan, "20 Best Last Lines in Movie History," Screen Rant, October 10, 2022, https://screenrant.com/best-last-movie-lines-quotes-ever/

14. Wilson Chapman, "Martin Scorsese's Favorite Movies: 84 Films the Director Wants You to See," IndieWire, July 15, 2024, https://www.indiewire.com/gallery/martin-scorsese-favorite-films-movies/

15. Mekado Murphy, "10 Movies that Capture The Essence of New York." *New York Times*, June 3, 2023, https://www.

nytimes.com/2023/06/03/movies/new-york-city-movies-tribeca.html

16. Ibid.

17. Caitlin Morton, "49 Movies That Will Transport You to New York City." *Conde Nast Traveler*, May 13, 2020. https://www.cntraveler.com/gallery/best-new-york-city-movies

18. Christopher Orr, "'Ted Lasso' Recap, Season 2 Episode 9: Beard Has a Late Night." *New York Times,* September 17, 2021 https://www.nytimes.com/2021/09/17/arts/television/ted-lasso-recap-season-2-episode-9-beard-has-a-late-night.html

19. Warren Barrett, "The Meaning Behind The Song: People Who Died by Jim Carroll Band." Musician Wages, September 16, 2023, https://www.musicianwages.com/the-meaning-behind-the-song-people-who-died-by-jim-carroll-band/

20. Ben Tanzer, "Ben Tanzer Recommends the *Basketball Diaries.*" TNBCC's The Next Best Book Blog, November 11, 2014, https://thenextbestbookblog.blogspot.com/2014/11/ben-tanzer-recommends-basketball-diaries.html

21. Kevin Tschierse, "Martin Scorsese: 5 things that make him great." DW, November 17, 2022, https://www.dw.com/en/martin-scorsese-5-things-that-make-him-a-great-filmmaker/a-63773313

22. Roger Ebert, "The time is three a.m. Do you know where your sanity is?" RogerEbert.com, January 14, 2009, https://www.rogerebert.com/reviews/after-hours-1985-1

23. Nick Ripatrazone, "30 Years Later, Scorsese Makes His Silence." Lithub, January 17, 2017, https://lithub.com/30-years-later-scorsese-makes-his-silence/

24.Lauren Eggert-Crowe,"With Fire In Her Heart."*Los Angeles Review of Books*, August 7, 2015. https://lareviewofbooks. org/article/with-fire-in-her-heart-hollywood-notebook/

25. Patrick Gibbs, "Film Review: *Creed III.*" *Slug Magazine*, March 9, 2023, https://www.slugmag.com/arts/film-arts/ film-reviews/creed-iii/